Biogra

Joy Buolamwini

FIGHT FOR HUMANITY IN THE AGE OF AI

TABLE OF CONTENTS

CHAPTER 1: DAUGHTER OF ART AND SCIENCE

CHAPTER 2: THE FUTURE FACTORY

CHAPTER 3: BREAK THE ALABASTER

CHAPTER 4: SHIELD READY

CHAPTER 5: DEFAULTS ARE NOT NEUTRAL

CHAPTER 6: FACIAL RECOGNITION TECHNOLOGIES

CHAPTER 7: POWER SHADOWS

CHAPTER 8: CRAWLING THROUGH DATA

CHAPTER 9: GENDER SHADES

CHAPTER 10: DESERTED DESSERTS

CHAPTER 11: AI, AIN'T I A WOMAN?

CHAPTER 12: POET VS. GOLIATH IN THE WILD

CHAPTER 13: BROOKLYN TENANTS

CHAPTER 14: TESTIFY

CHAPTER 15: BETTING ON CODED BIAS

CHAPTER 16: COSTS OF INCLUSION AND EXCLUSION

CHAPTER 17: CUPS OF HOPE

CHAPTER 1

DAUGHTER OF ART AND SCIENCE

I am the daughter of science and art. Frema the Akan, my mother, was the first artist I knew. I sat next to her as a child while she filled canvas after canvas with vibrant colours and brought innovative ideas to life. Drawing books, portfolios, imitation fruits, and flowers were among the art items that littered our garage. My mother studied human cardiac diseases. Her work, she explained, was intended to move people to feel healing, to see the divine, to be enthralled and swept into another state of consciousness. I would watch her intently, pondering the next stroke to apply to an expanding work of art. Her experiments and unfinished pieces were a continual presence in my life. Seeing her sculpt, paint, draw, and chisel out art was a sensory overload for me. Her four-foot-tall paintings towered over me, and the aromas of charcoal and turpentine enticed my nostrils. Our world was an open invitation to experiment with artistic expression. I quickly had sketchbooks full of whatever had piqued my interest at the time—ramps, skateboards, mustangs, animated characters, guitars, and amplifiers. My mother's encouraging voice, a constant echo, gave me the confidence to pursue my abilities and my curiosity. However, artistic endeavours were not the only ones that occurred during my upbringing.

Dr. John Buolamwini, my father, was the first scientist I met. He worked on subjects that were difficult for me to pronounce: medical chemistry, pharmaceutical sciences, and computer-aided drug development utilising neural nets. Trips to his lab were entertaining and full of stuff not to touch, a lesson I frequently learned the hard way. Chalk is not edible. Dry ice causes burns. As I walked to his office, I noticed corridors lined with scientific posters and him waving to colleagues and students. Then, if I was lucky, I got to play on one of the computers while Daddy worked on the newest grant, research article, or other desk job. I trailed him like a shadow as he headed to the freezer in his lab. He donned purple gloves, took out a tray, and set it on a lab bench. My dad smiled as I fought to get the large gloves on my hands. Once I was safe, he placed a pipette in my hand and gently pressed my right thumb with his. While my eyes expanded with curiosity and his beard tickled my head, liquid drops soaked the cancer cells beneath our cupped hands. More PCs sat next to the lab bench. He would show me machines associated with notions such as flow cytometry. I'd look at the squiggles on the computers, which I subsequently learned were graphs. He, like my mother, was conducting studies that required courageous curiosity to ask unanswered questions. But, while my mother inquired about colours, my father inquired about cells. In the midst of their excursions, I began to ask computer-related inquiries. For example, how did the images I saw in scholarly articles come to be? They appeared to be abstract paintings to me. My father showed me the program that would generate these graphics with ringlets and rods of vivid reds and blues indicating different protein structures on his massive Silicon Graphics processors. The purpose of feeding the cells, developing medical medications on a computer, executing all the tests, and studying the squiggles was to treat patients suffering from illnesses ranging from heart disease to breast cancer. He showed me the software to expose me to chemistry, but I became increasingly fascinated by the machines themselves. I rapidly discovered pre-installed games like Doom and Cycle. I sat and listened to the beeps and whirrs of a dial-up connection. In that workplace, I launched Netscape, my first foray into what I subsequently learned was the internet. As a result of being surrounded by art and science from a young age, I was encouraged to investigate, to ask questions, to dare to change what appeared fixed, and to see the artist's and scientist's quest for truth as common companions.

My parents taught me that the unknown was an opportunity to learn, not a dangerous realm to be avoided. Ignorance was a stepping stone to deeper levels of comprehension. They would eventually become tired of my never-ending questions; after engaging my curiosity for a while, my mother would sometimes bring me back down to earth with a soft "Why has a long tail..." elongating her words as she spoke. In addition to my parents, I turned to television for information. My parents, who were first-generation immigrants settling in Oxford, Mississippi, wouldn't allow me to watch commercials because they wanted to protect me from the materialism that looked to be the backbone of American culture. "You will never find your worth in things," they forewarned. However, they pushed me to watch educational shows, thus PBS became our household's preferred television station. I soon began to look forward to shows like Nature, National Geographic, Nova, and Scientific American Frontier. One episode in particular left an indelible impression on me. I remember watching a robot part when I was approximately nine years old. The host of the show went to the Massachusetts Institute of Technology. He chatted with a graduate student named Cynthia Breazeal about her research on "social robots." Unlike the industrial robots I'd seen before, which were monstrous machines assigned to duties like pounding out sheet metal, her social robot was focused on connection and communication rather than work. She sat beside Kismet, a bright and complicated web of metal and cables topped with captivating eyes, moving ears, and a mischievous smile. I was amazed the instant I saw the machine appear to come to life. Could I create anything similar to Kismet? Could I go to MIT, which served as the setting for so many of the science and technology shows I watched? I knew then that I wanted to attend MIT and work as a robotics engineer. I was blissfully oblivious of any obstacles or prerequisites. I had additional computing inquiries, nourished in the incubator of youthful possibilities by the conviction that I might become anything I envisioned. Learning how to program machines to do what I wanted was my first step toward making robots. I discovered various types of programming languages to guide machines. I began by learning the fundamentals of HTML and CSS in order to create a website. These programming languages were structured and formatted. HTML enabled me to specify the elements I wanted to appear on a webpage, such as a block of text, a button, or an image. CSS allowed me to control the appearance of these elements, from the colour of the text to the amount of space between them. Each programming language had its own set of rules for instructing a machine. I soon found myself employing these talents to code websites for my high school sports teams in order to earn some extra money or barter. Even though I was only a benchwarmer on the basketball team, I didn't have to pay for a uniform or sneakers. I wanted to go beyond websites and learn how to develop games like the ones I used to play with my brother on his Nintendo 64 or Tony Hawk Pro Skater 2, which I adored on my Sony PlayStation. So I learnt Java, another programming language. The concept of an algorithm was presented to me here. In its most basic form, an algorithm is a set of instructions used to accomplish a given task. I would write code that followed a logical order to move my character around the screen. For example, if the user presses the left arrow, move the character to the left on the screen. As I would later discover, algorithms like this would serve as the foundation for increasingly sophisticated and dynamic systems.

In college, I followed my desire to work on robotics. I was working on social robots by my third year at the Georgia Institute of Technology in Atlanta. Andrea Thomaz, one of the teachers I worked with, was a former student of Cynthia Breazeal. And, to my surprise, when I began working on Thomaz's robot Simon, I discovered that the code that powered it had descended from the CREATURES code library that formerly animated Kismet. My task with Simon was to see if I could get the robot to connect socially with a person. I finally decided to start on a project named Peekaboo Simon. The goal was for the robot to play a simple turn-taking game with a human partner, comparable to what a parent might do with a small child. The overarching goal of this experiment was to investigate if we could have a robot play social games with young children and analyse how they responded and behaved during those encounters, assisting in the diagnosis of early developmental delays or even early indicators of autism. This type of early detection could assist a youngster in receiving the essential assistance as soon as possible. To play this game, I'd need Simon the robot to detect a human face and turn its head toward the person. This was my first experience with face detection. I was learning about the topic of computer vision in class, which enables machines to sense the world using digital cameras and then utilise software on the camera input to execute a variety of jobs, such as detecting a ball, a block, or, in my case, a human face. When an object was spotted, a rectangle, sometimes known as a bounding box, appeared on the image to show where it was. I stumbled into a problem while working on the project: Peekaboo doesn't work if your partner doesn't see you, and Simon the robot was having trouble detecting my face. I'd switch on all the lights, move my head in all directions, and bemoan the fact that the bounding box that was meant to represent the location of my face appeared only occasionally. In desperation, I enlisted the help of my roommate, a cheerful southern lady with brilliant red hair, green eyes, and freckled complexion. Because the software worked on her fair skin, I was able to continue with the assignment. I didn't think much of the experience because my major goal was to finish the project, and it wasn't the first time cameras had failed me. When I was taken outside of studio lights, my childhood photos revealed less than flattering images. In several of these images, you could only see the whites of my eyes and teeth, not the rest of my face.

As I explored college, I had other interests other than computer vision research. I dabbled in entrepreneurship. In 2011, Sarah and Elizabeth, two of my classmates, and I competed in an international competition and were chosen to represent the United States in Hong Kong. Our objective was to build a platform that would allow musicians to jam with anyone, anywhere, at any time. While we did not go past the first round, we made the most of our time in Hong Kong. We danced hard to dubstep at night and visited Hong Kong Science Park during the day, the throbbing pulse of the night before still ringing in our heads. During our visit to the science park, I met another Kismet descendant. Autom was a healthcare social robot established by Corey Kidd, another former Cynthia Breazeal student who had gone to Hong Kong to start a company centred on integrating social robots into healthcare. The technology was leaving the lab and into the real world. Corey and his colleagues demonstrated the robot, and I offered to test it. I looked into Autom's camera eyes, but the system couldn't recognize my face. Corey appeared taken aback. I suspected I was aware of the problem. We started talking business, and I discovered that Corey was utilising the same facial detection software that I had used on Simon. I had the same difficulty thousands of miles away from my dorm room in Atlanta, but I didn't think much of it. There was still more dancing to be done, and more people from all around the world to meet. After finishing my computer science degree at Georgia Tech, I went to Zambia as a Fulbright scholar to teach young people how to code before moving on to Oxford University, where I would return to academia and technology. I had a talk with my favourite scientist near the end of my tenure as a Rhodes Scholar at Oxford. My father, who is always concerned about academic credentials, reminded me that I had not yet received my PhD and should consider applying to graduate school. His call reminded me of my family's legacy. My father came before my mother's father, who received his PhD in England in 1969, decades before I was born in 1990. When graduate school application season arrived, I remembered my childhood fantasies and the appeal of a robot named Kismet on the family television screen, and I applied to only one place.

CHAPTER 2
THE FUTURE FACTORY

Some wishes are granted. After weeks of nervously watching my email, Ethan Zuckerman, the director of the Center for Civic Media, sent me an offer letter for a research assistantship at the MIT Media Lab. When I called him, he greeted me in Twi, my first language, and I was impressed by his efforts to make me feel welcome. Aside from Ethan's passion, the Media Lab had a mythological air for me as the "Future Factory," a place where designers, scientists, and engineers came to dream and construct possibilities for how life may be. Everything from social robots, LEGO Mindstorms, and visual programming languages to Guitar Hero, digital ink, and early sketches of autonomous vehicles were developed here. During a campus tour before accepting MIT's offer, I spoke with a professor who told me, "If what you are thinking of making already exists, go elsewhere."

The prospect of being at the forefront of future technical discoveries piqued my interest. When I joined in 2015, the MIT Media Lab was composed of over twenty smaller labs, including Opera of the Future, Lifelong Kindergarten, and Tangible Media, all of which were led by well-known faculty members such as Cynthia Breazeal. Though most of the groups were concerned with future worlds, the Center for Civic Media, or Civic Media for short, was concerned with the impact of technology on society today. Civic Media claimed that the heart of technology must be placed at the core of society. This made us curious in an environment that was otherwise focused on conquering society's restrictions. Despite my aim to create futuristic technology, my previous work has been centred on technologies with immediate real-world applicability.

While I was excited to be at MIT, under the supervision of a supervisor who wanted to make me feel like I belonged, I remained an outsider. My first semester on campus coincided with the lab's 30th anniversary, and festivities were in full flow. Martha Stewart and the magicians Penn and Teller had travelled to town as part of the celebrations. Their presence was appropriate for a setting described by the leadership as animated by enchantment, mystery, and mischief. We received thirtieth-anniversary dress shirts from Ministry of Supply, a recent MIT spinout company that used astronaut textiles, as students. Because the brand didn't make women's clothing at the time, I had to settle with an extra small men's dress shirt. The bulk of Media Lab faculty and students were men back then. Nonetheless, this wrinkle-free and stain-resistant white dress shirt became a cherished cornerstone of my Media Lab outfit, which I wore over more bright red and yellow V-neck shirts. I was used to adding dashes of colour to otherwise bleached views by this point. The Media Lab, like the dress shirt, was kept stain-free. I recall passing into the atrium one day and seeing a man apply white paint on little scuff marks on otherwise beautiful walls. With this kind of attention to detail, it's no wonder that the Media Lab was also an architectural gem, appearing more like the headquarters of a cutting-edge technological firm than a normal academic structure comprising classrooms and offices. There were tantalising exhibits of self-pedalling tricycles, metal origami blocks, and screens cycling through video demos around the premises. A room-sized food computer prototype was one of my favourites. It looked like a greenhouse with different regions for different plants, and each plant patch was equipped with sensors that could warn the gardeners when anything needed to be done. I ordered an Uber to take me to campus one night early in the semester, but after only a few minutes in the car, the driver decided he didn't want to drive me. When he threatened to call the cops if I didn't get out, I walked toward MIT. A patrol car drove up behind me on my way there, rolling slowly nearby in warning. Was this all in my brain, or was I not really accepted in Cambridge? I had security at the lab, or so I thought.

As a fulbright fellow in zambia in 2013, I collaborated with young people to develop mobile applications to disseminate knowledge about women's rights. This project aimed to increase the number of women and people of colour who pursue careers in computer science and software engineering. This simultaneous curiosity in who was generating technology and how technology could be used to tackle real-world problems carried over into my MIT study. When I was considering which courses to pursue, I sought advice from Ethan. "Take a class that builds your skills, take a class that deepens your knowledge, and take a class that is just for fun." With this motivation, I eagerly enrolled in a fun course that would change the course of my life: Science Fabrication. The seminar was taught by Dan Novy, a Hollywood special-effects guru, and Joost Bonsen, a student entrepreneurship accelerator, and it was primarily focused on inventing fantastical futuristic technologies.

So, in my first year at the Future Factory, I began working on the Aspire Mirror, a whimsical contraption inspired by stories my parents told me about Ananse the trickster. My white mask was still sitting on my desk, a constant reminder of my most recent contact with the coded gaze. I ignored my unease, like I had with the Uber driver and the Cambridge cops, and moved on to the next semester. I collaborated with a group of students on a project called Upbeat Walls for another course. We were a diverse group that included a musician, an MIT Sloan School of Management business student, an undergraduate studying computer science, a Media Lab master's student with engineering talents, and me, the resident computer programmer. We began with a provocative question: What if you could paint walls with your smile? From there, imagine your face as a paintbrush, with each stroke producing its own musical melody. Over the course of a week, we worked on a prototype.

We had a system that employed facial tracking technology to allow a user to come up to our little wall, move their face, and have digital strokes emerge on the wall by the time demo day arrived. Each stroke would be accompanied by a sound, including a beatboxing mix I had created.[*] As with the Aspire Mirror, the technology functioned best for people with lighter skin during the demo. The coded stare persisted.

Even as I tried to provide an escape from the evils and worries of everyday life, I couldn't avoid the recurring problems with the technology I was developing. The software libraries I used were not designed for folks with darker skin like me. I had encountered these challenges as an undergraduate, face to face with Autumn in Hong Kong, and now they had reappeared. Despite all of the advances in artificial intelligence over the years, the problem had not been resolved. Despite the fact that I had moved the face tracking software to a different domain, the fundamental difficulties clung to me like a persistent bug.

CHAPTER 3
BREAK THE ALABASTER

Change was in the air as I returned to MIT for the start of my second year. The 2016 presidential campaign was in full swing, and the Georgetown Law Center on Privacy and Technology had just released a big new research on police use of face recognition technology. According to the analysis, the faces of one in every two persons, or at least 117 million people in the United States, appeared in databases that could be examined without warrants by police departments employing unaudited facial recognition technology. I could no longer convince myself that the problems I had repeatedly encountered with computer vision technologies were unimportant. It was one thing if I couldn't paint a picture with my smile, but if someone was mistaken for a criminal suspect and wrongfully jailed or worse, the stakes were plainly high. At the same time, I was dealing with the intersection of privilege and oppression while living in very opulent surroundings for a graduate student. As a master's student at MIT, I had the good fortune to become a resident tutor at Harvard. There, I assisted students with fellowship applications and mentored a small group of sophomores. I received housing, a meal plan, access to Harvard facilities, and transportation in exchange. My apartment was on the corner of Bow and Arrow streets, inside Westmorly Court's oak-panelled walls. A grey stone etching between two sets of brick-lined steps outside the building boldly stated that the spot had been US President Franklin Delano Roosevelt's student lodgings. It was only a five-minute walk to the Charles River and an even shorter walk to the blue Harvard shuttle that took me to MIT every morning. Harvard dining hall workers went on strike in the fall of 2016 to demand improved working conditions and remuneration. From my room, I could hear them screaming "No justice, no peace," and I could see their signs from my window. I nodded in time with the music. Change was permeating the university as well. Karen Brennan, a Media Lab graduate who is now a Harvard professor teaching an MIT course, asked my classmates and me, "What will you do with your privilege?" Maybe it was time for me to speak up about the problems I was seeing with the new face-based technologies being employed by police. But I was still undecided. I wanted to be a maker rather than a critic. The white mask incident had been upsetting, but I didn't want people to believe I was making everything about race, or that I was unappreciative of rare and hard-won opportunities. Speaking up had repercussions. Ethan had also encouraged me to talk more clearly about the political consequences of my job. He urged me to make stronger links between the dearth of representation of women and people of colour in technology and white supremacy and patriarchy. "And Joy's work is looking at inequalities and power asymmetries in computer science education," he would say during group meetings. "Do you have anything else to say?" I declined because I was uncomfortable with this framing. "Umm, I am just focused on teaching people how to code apps they care about." Graduate school was difficult enough. Why deal with the stigma and extra scrutiny of being a power dynamics gadfly?

In some ways, I got into computer science to get away from the tangle of multi headed -isms like racism, sexism, classism, and others. In my personal life, I was acutely conscious of discrimination. I just wanted to enjoy the fun of coding and create futuristic technology, or even real-world applications focused on health, without having to worry about removing -isms. I also didn't want to be a bother. Despite all evidence to the contrary, I wanted to think that technology might be apolitical. And I hoped that if I could continue to see technology and my work as apolitical, I wouldn't have to act or speak out in ways that may put me in danger. Plus, I feared that focusing too much on these ever-present characteristics would make me bitter and sap the joy that had led me to seek male-dominated fields in the first place. I believed that if you worked hard enough, you could transcend the -isms or at least diminish them to the point that their weight didn't dramatically affect your life trajectory. Meritocracy must be true in some way. Hadn't I gotten into MIT? I wanted to cling to that fantasy rather than face the harder facts. When I was in high school, I recall arguing with my father about the importance of affirmative action. I didn't think it was essential at the time because I had been somewhat shielded from the ways in which women and people of colour were being denied chances. My father pushed me to watch Tony Brown's Journal and a PBS women's roundtable to help me grow out of my juvenile ignorance. My qualifications stood alone, regardless of colour or gender. I had no doubt that I was qualified, and I didn't want others to think that I was given opportunities solely because of my ethnicity and gender. It came down to personal pride at the end of the day. The older I became, the more I realised how fortunate I was to have had access to art galleries and science labs at such a young age. My exposure to science and technology was an outlier, and exceptionalism would not alter the social fabric.

Exceptionalism also held the risk of tokenism, which allowed systemic flaws to be overlooked by focusing on a few examples of alleged success while disregarding the more prevalent story. I was frequently used as a progress poster, appearing in college marketing materials and conference brochures to demonstrate that change was possible. Still, I understood that if the cards had been dealt differently, my life could have taken a very different turn. Many dedicated, intelligent people could be in my position if they had similar opportunities. I had to admit that numerous things outside of my control influenced my capacity to take advantage of educational opportunities. In many ways, I was born fortunate. This acknowledgement does not diminish my efforts, but rather broadens the discussion to include more than one individual and more about the society we have built. And perhaps, given my position, I had an obligation to speak up. Perhaps Ethan was correct. I needed to discover my voice.

Natalie Rusk from the Lifelong Kindergarten organisation contacted me about a reading at the Harvard Book Store around this time. Cathy O'Neil came to town to promote her new book, Weapons of Math Destruction. Because I lived around the corner from the Harvard Book Store, I strolled over to the book talk after supper in the Adams House dining hall, which was now short-staffed due to the ongoing protests. An imposing woman with short blue hair sat on a stool at the back of the establishment. She discussed how data was used to sort and manipulate people. She emphasised how mathematical models were being exploited as smoke screens to conceal inequalities. She illustrated this unfairness with instances from the 2008 mortgage crisis and fraudulent advertisements for for-profit colleges. During the question and answer session, I introduced myself and mentioned that I had noticed some of what she was talking about in recent work I had done with face detection models.

Though she was unfamiliar with the computer vision sector, our chat made me feel like I wasn't the only one obsessed with glimpses of the coded gaze. While I had a residential community at Harvard, brilliant lab mates at MIT, and someone I was seeing who led me outside of the Cambridge bubble to spend time across the Charles River in Roxbury, my growing interest in the dangers of data-driven technology left me intellectually alone. I purchased Cathy's bright yellow book, which was inscribed with her autograph. I no longer felt alone in my investigation of algorithmic prejudice as I read the book chapter by chapter. I may have an ally if I were to be a gadfly.

Civic-minded elders and leaders expanded my understanding about technology and society. We would have regulars at weekly group meetings open to the public, in addition to our lab staff and graduate students, including retirees like Saul and Anne, who would dispute some of the graduate students' idealistic project ideas.

"What happens to the data you are collecting about people's location?"

"How would someone without a smartphone be able to benefit from what you are proposing?"

Visitors would include activists, former political prisoners, and others who had served on the front lines of conflict zones. Esra'a Al Shafei, who came from Bahrain and spoke about the platforms she had created, such as Mideast Youth, which allowed music to develop and enabled gay youth to find community, captivated me. She spoke of her pals, fellow campaigners who had been imprisoned for their convictions. She also discussed the problems of fundraising and how foundations would direct her to learn from young Western guys establishing platforms that were unrelated to the job she and her colleagues had been doing for many years. Visitors from organisations such as the Robert Wood Johnson Foundation would come to see how our Media Cloud program, which was designed to follow media outlets from all around the world, was capturing information about specific themes such as mental health.

Our diverse mix of guests allowed me to witness how the Center for Civic Media used technology to bring together decision-makers and community members for meaningful conversations that eventually examined the power dynamics that influenced decision-making. Yes, a technical tool may help us collect data, give supporting evidence, and even answer questions we couldn't previously, but this was done to hold decision-makers accountable or to connect others who cared about related problems. Still, I couldn't shake the idea that it could be preferable for me to modify my research focus. I had originally pursued the idea of stimulating civic imagination through mobile app creation for my thesis, and I had already put in significant work: After raising funds, renting a studio for three days of shooting, and working with an editor for months, I built an online course. During the summer following my first year at the Media Lab, I offered seminars with a local school. But I couldn't get rid of the idea that there was something more I should be doing.

As a result, I reached out to senior graduate students for advice. "If I were you, I would not change directions now; you just spent a year on a project and you only have one more year left." "Working on topics like gender bias will generate a lot of backlash." You can be pigeonholed in ways that are detrimental to your career." And they said "Your advisor is not focused on AI; you are going to have to learn so much on your own if you go down this path." The older graduates provided me with sound advice. However, I was tempted to take the greater risk.

Pole vaulting was my favourite track event in high school. Not only did I appreciate the physical challenge, which needed sprinter speed, thrower strength, and gymnast body awareness, but it also provided me with a metaphor for life. Pole vaulting taught me early on that where you fix your gaze is where you eventually land. Staring straight at the bar frequently resulted in clashing with it or barely making it over. To perform a spectacular vault, you had to look past the bar and up into the sky. Shifting your focus from the bar to the stars allows your body to follow a more expansive vision. The older graduate students at MIT who had advised me were staring out the window as they tried to complete. I still had some time. I wanted to gaze at the stars.

Ethan's office had a window that looked out onto a courtyard and another that looked into our lab space. Fellow graduate students may see if he was available for a conversation through the in-facing window. The blinds were up that day, and I could see he was free, so I approached. I let out a deep sigh as I sat on the black futon Ethan used to sleep on when he remained late at the lab. For a time, I fidgeted with my hands and remained mute. Then, in a lengthy monologue, I stated that I was increasingly drawn to facial recognition technologies and that I felt the topic may have a significant influence. I wasn't sure what I wanted to focus my research on, but I couldn't shake the feeling that there was some work in the space I was supposed to do.

He gazed at me with sympathetic eyes. "You know, it's OK not to have all the answers, Joy."

I averted my gaze so he wouldn't notice my tears.

"I know."

It was simpler to be confrontational than it was to be vulnerable. After some thought, he told me that as someone who will always have a lot of hobbies, I would have to decide what should be side projects. He suggested that I keep this new work as one of my artistic investigations in order to maintain the momentum of the work I was currently producing.

CHAPTER 4
SHIELD READY

I met two people from the Collaboratorium, an organisation focusing on creative collaborations, by coincidence while wandering through the Media Lab's third-floor atrium. I told them about my plan to make a short video regarding the concept of the coded gaze. They were in town for a few days and decided to volunteer to film scenes for the little documentary. I returned home to get a bright red shirt. Given that this was a special occasion, I even put on some makeup, which is unusual in my usual rush-out-the-door routine. We convened late at night at the Civic table in the middle, cleared away chairs, and improvised illumination. The cameraman connected a few extension cables, stood on a table, and stretched just enough to attach the plug for an above light supported by exposed pipes. Sands Fish, my lab colleague, had lately installed a workbench. I read the Do Not Touch sign to mean that outsiders should not touch it. The exposed wood chip workstation was topped with a turquoise gridded mat that served as a small yet eye-catching stage for my laptop. The coded gaze art staff collected our materials and organised last-minute posters still wet with black ink on the day of the event, leaving proof on the fingers of everyone who helped organise the show. The Aspire Mirror was described by one commenter. Another explained the relationship between human bias and coded bias. The largest poster was my personal favourite. The word "Algorithmic Justice League" was printed in white ink—the name I was using to characterise the work I was doing. The name is based on the "justice league" flag, which many others have used to fight for societal reform since the start of the twentieth century—decades before DC Comics used the phrase for their fictitious worlds. Civic organisations used the term "justice league" in the early twentieth century to fight for women's suffrage. Hundreds of justice-related groups continue to draw on this legacy today. Real-world justice leagues inspire the conviction that in the face of tyranny, persecution, and erasure, we may choose to resist and give paths to liberation. Following this banner, I positioned the burgeoning work I was doing with the Algorithmic Justice League. I set up an interactive presentation of the Upbeat Walls project for the event, where guests could try to paint walls with their grins if their faces were identified. As visitors began to trickle into the exhibition, I began to detect a pattern. A person with fair skin would test the interactive Upbeat Walls, and their face would be identified and music would begin to play. Someone with darker skin might try unsuccessfully until they donned the white mask I had placed on the table. "It works so well for me, I didn't even think it wouldn't work for someone else," a fair-skinned person said. "Dang, the machines can't see us either?" said someone with a darker complexion.

Without seeing another person struggle with the Upbeat Walls approach, the individual who had used it concluded that it worked for everyone. When they discovered that wasn't the case, they were reinforced in their newfound understanding by watching a video about the coded gaze. And the person for whom the system failed to function properly concluded that it was the machine's fault, not theirs. This was not the result of user error. There was something more going on under the hood, and that was the focus of the entire display. Donald Trump was elected President of the United States on November 9, 2016, just a few days after the art show. While some of my boyhood friends in Memphis, Tennessee, rejoiced, there was a tangible sense of disappointment in the streets of Cambridge. Our group, which had previously been a curiosity in the Future Factory, was now a destination. People from other lab groups began to flock to our Wednesday afternoon sessions, which were open to the public. These guests were inspired to consider the role of technology in today's society, and they came to see what they could learn from our work. I assisted in bringing out more and more folding chairs to accommodate everyone who had joined us. The tables that had formerly supported Ethan in his sorrow over funding were now home to the whole Media Lab community. Students working on new user interfaces, gene editing tools, and unusual musical instruments attended our gatherings. An undertone murmured, "What is the value of the work I am doing?" and "Can we use the power and access we have at a place like Media Lab to change society?" We were gathered to have a safe space to express our anxieties and hopes. Ethan modelled for me what it looked like to hold space for others, no matter where they were on their journey of political awareness, to come and be heard, to ask questions, to express doubts, and to find community through our open lab space. How could I accentuate issues I was witnessing with AI, which was now increasingly in the hands of a government that was swiftly losing my faith, in an age of rising populism?

But I knew I needed to reach more people than those who had seen the MFA exhibit, and I wanted to tell my narrative of coding in a white mask and the increasing use of AI to make key life decisions like who gets employed or dismissed. I'd soon have another stage to act on. I discovered about a TEDxBeaconStreet event in mid-November, and while speakers had already been chosen, the organiser, John Werner, was a familiar figure around the Media Lab. The schedule for the main stage was already full, but John offered a spot on the TEDxYouth@BeaconStreet program. It wasn't what I had hoped for, but it was enough to get me started. I focused on my presentation and then emailed John, pleading with him to give me a shot on the main stage. He connected me with a speaking coach and materials for giving a compelling presentation. After refining my speech and attending a few practice sessions, John invited me to the main stage, as long as I felt comfortable given the tight time frame. He warned me that instead of the usual three months, I would only have a few weeks to prepare. This was the invitation I had been looking forward to. I agreed to take on the challenge. On the day of the event, John met me and two emotional support guests. They had been my practice audience the day before. They could repeat some of the sections of my speech with me by the time I memorised it. I chose to recycle some of the MFA exhibition features by bringing one of the newly minted shields with AJL inscribed on the front on top of a mischievous smirk. It was finally showtime. A technician backstage fitted me with a "flesh colour" microphone. The delicate pink tint clashed with my sparkling milk chocolate skin. I inquired whether they had anything darker. They did not do so. As the speaker in front of me stepped offstage, I could hear a murmur from behind the curtain. I gripped a boxy clicker for my slides, my palm slightly sweaty. I stepped onto the stage, taking a deep breath. I walked up and began after finding my speaker mark on the floor. "An unseen force is rising...what I refer to as the coded gaze." It's spreading like wildfire."

The crowd leaned in as I discussed how algorithmic bias affects everything from who gets recruited or fired to how much you spend for a product. When an AI system serves one group better than another, this is referred to as algorithmic bias. You have encountered algorithmic bias if you were denied employment because an AI system screened out individuals who attended women's colleges. Looking down, I noticed that the timer had run out. I sprinted to my final slide as time ran out. "So I invite you to join me in making a world where technology works for everyone, not just some of us...Will you fight alongside me?" Yes, there was a standing ovation. The momentum was building. At this point in my MIT academic career, I began to accept what I could do with the luxury of being at a high-profile institution. Rather than feeling as if I was abandoning my idealism of working on technology to avoid hard reality, I could understand how my childhood interests might coexist with my growing purpose of researching detrimental prejudice in technology. My life path and educational options were beginning to make sense to me. I felt emboldened to ask even more awkward questions about the machines that had once captivated me. WITH MY SHIELD ON MY shoulder, I rushed to the Media Lab. Jogging to our great glass elevators, I frantically pushed the sixth-floor button to make it in time for Crit Day. My fellow second-year master's students were exploring so many varied ideas that touched on the thematic trifecta of new technology, aesthetic appeal, and social impact. Nicole L'Huillier, a Chilean musician in the Opera of the Future group, presented on tectonic music to explore new kinds of musical experiences that blended sonic sensations with touch. Stick your head in a box, hold an orb, and feel pressure corresponding to the sound waves that were playing. Udayan Umapathi, who grew up in a small town in India, was from the Tangible Media group. He worked on a project called Droplet IO that allowed the movement of water droplets to be programmed. Using electrical signals, a droplet could be moved precisely to any location and combined with other droplets. From an artistic perspective it could be used to create stunning visualisations, while from a commercial angle the technology was poised to revolutionise microfluidics, the precise manipulation of fluids. Instead of using disposable pipettes that had a negative climate impact, chemical reagents could be mixed with precision, ushering in a new age of digital microfluidics. I was thankful that he presented after me. In the Camera Culture group, focused on making the invisible visible, Tristen Swedish, who often sported a red beard, was working on eyeSelfie, through which a specialised lens was attached to a smartphone and images were processed with an app that would assist in the diagnosis of eye conditions. The device and accessory would allow for telemedicine in rural areas with limited access to optometrists and ophthalmologists. This work reminded me of the work on trachoma I had done as an undergraduate in Ethiopia.

I began my presentation with two videos. In the first one I stare into a camera and say, "Hi, camera, can you see my face?" I pause. Nothing. "You can see my friend's face." The video cuts to the face of my friend Mary Maggic, a Chinese American speculative artist. Her face is quickly detected. "What about my face?" The camera returns to my face. I make an exaggerated pout on camera, drawing laughter from the audience. "I have a mask." I put on the white mask, which is immediately detected. "Can you see my mask?" The laughter shifts to audible gasps. On the black screen, three white words linger: "The Coded Gaze."

I then presented another video. In this one I show a person walking in front of a car that is presumed to be self-driving. The car does not slow down and instead collides with the person. I used these videos to tease the idea that computer vision technology was further infiltrating our lives and that the consequences of not being detected by a computer vision system were not just for chuckles but could in fact be grave. The AI techniques used to detect a face were similar to the techniques used to detect a body. I wanted to show that my focus on faces was only a starting point, and the implications of the work would reach beyond just the face space. An advantage of focusing on an area like computer vision was the ability to demonstrate the kinds of errors being made by a given system. With the white mask example, viewers could see the difference in performance between Mary Maggic and me without a lengthy explanation. Showing and not just telling about computer vision, I reasoned, would allow for powerful depictions of the notion of algorithmic bias and the coded gaze. I call this approach of showing technical failures, to allow others to bear witness to ways technology could be harmful, evocative audits. The focus of my Media Lab master's work would be "Unmasking Algorithmic Bias." I ended the presentation with a fist pump and raised the AJL shield.

Ethan shouted, "The shield is backwards." I turned it around, ready to field questions. When the presentations were finished, a woman who had been sitting near the front approached me with a question. It was Cynthia Breazeal. Years after having Cynthia's robot Kismet spark my curiosity, I stood in front of a woman I had long admired, engaging in conversation that had once been but a distant dream.

CHAPTER 5
DEFAULTS ARE NOT NEUTRAL

I entered "TED.com" on my keyboard while sitting on a purple couch outside Ethan's office. My Beacon Street talk was featured on the home page. I grabbed a screenshot to remember the moment, forwarded the joyful news to my friends, and continuously reloaded the page to see how many people had seen it. The editors chose the title "How I am Fighting Bias in Algorithms" to present my work to the public. The views continued to rise in thousands, ten thousands, and hundred thousands increments. The video would be watched over a million times. Everyone was paying attention. I began reading the comments. Some were nice, but not the ones I recalled. From rude comments like "the mask does not [sic] have to be white you are just ugly" to others disputing the existence of algorithmic bias, my initial elation quickly turned to worry. Was speaking up about these issues going to result in constant verbal abuse and doubts? The spotlight glows and burns at the same time. The insults were nothing new to me, yet they still sting. As much as I wanted to respond angrily, I realised that doing so would be detrimental to others who were truly curious or uneducated. "Does this woman not understand how cameras work...when photographing darker skin tones [sic], different settings and lighting must be used." "Lighter skin tones reflect light better," remarked one user. I intended to argue my point and demonstrate the intellectual case for algorithmic prejudice. The comments sparked the title "Algorithms aren't racist, your face is just too dark" for an article I published immediately after the TED spotlight. My white mask experience provided context for the possibility of racial bias in computer vision systems. My usage of bias was predicated on the premise of favouring or disadvantageous one group over another depending on race. People have prejudices, of course, but as one commentator put it, "there is no bias on maths algorithms [sic]." It was widely assumed that these mathematical systems produce objective conclusions; after all, one plus one equals two. Machines were thought to be immune to the cultural biases that beset us humans. My experiences had taught me otherwise. But as I began to talk about algorithmic bias with more individuals, I was frequently confronted with variants of this hushed, and sometimes not-so-hushed, question: Isn't the reason your face wasn't detected due to a lack of contrast given your dark complexion? (In other words, algorithms aren't racist—you just have too dark skin.)

Poor illumination is a major difficulty in the science of computer vision. In some cases, we reach the outer boundaries of the visible light spectrum. My concentration is not so much on the extreme instance as it is on the ordinary scenario. The TED.com demo depicts a real-world office scenario. A human eye can see my face and the face of my demonstration partner, Mary Maggic, but the human eye and the visual cortex that processes its input are significantly more sophisticated than a simple web camera. Even with the web camera, you can observe in the demo that my partner's face is neither overexposed to the point of being undetectable, nor is my face underexposed to the point of severe information loss. Without first taking a look at cameras and imaging technology, we cannot completely comprehend bias in computer vision. Even if cameras appear neutral, history tells a different narrative. To bring out desired colours, analog camera film was exposed using a particular chemical mixture. A standard was developed in order to calibrate the cameras and ensure that the desired colours were accurately displayed. The Shirley card, which was originally an image of a white woman intended to determine the optimal composition and exposure settings, became known as this standard. Because film cameras were calibrated using a light-skinned woman, the techniques developed did not function as well for people with darker skin. In fact, Kodak didn't introduce a new product that better caught a spectrum of browns and dark sepia tones until furniture and chocolate industries complained that the rich browns of their products weren't being effectively portrayed. Separating the appearance of milk chocolate from dark chocolate in advertising benefited chocolate-coloured people. Nonetheless, successive digital cameras inherited settings intended for light skin, resulting in a bigger group of photographs and films taken by cameras suited for only one segment of humanity: people with light skin. As we move into the area of computer vision, which increasingly relies on enormous datasets, we are confronted with a heritage of cameras and acquired images that inherit exclusion. That exclusion can mean that the features of someone with darker skin are less evident in a photograph or video, even when shot in favourable lighting conditions. The default options are not neutral. They frequently reflect the coded gaze—the preferences of people with the authority to choose which subjects to focus on. However, history has demonstrated that other systems can be created. The LDK camera series designed by Philips in the digital age expressly handled skin tone variation with two chips—one for processing darker tones and another for processing brighter tones. The Oprah Winfrey Show employed the LDK series for filming since the show's presenter and guests were aware of the need to properly reveal darker skin. Resistance persisted as I published the concept of the coded gaze and algorithmic prejudice. In impassioned letters and online comments, I read variations on "not EVERYTHING is racist" or "you cannot change the laws of physics." While there are physical constraints, as seen in the Kodak case, financial incentives can spur innovation. I was very careful to find an example of coding in a white mask where my lighter-skinned companion and I were in the same lighting circumstances and all of our face characteristics were apparent through the camera in the demo. Lighting and head attitude have an effect on how pixels appear in digital cameras. I chose the TED demo example to demonstrate that, while camera calibration has an impact, it is not the only factor. A critical component is how we educate machines to read input. Even in the case where my face was visible to the human eye through the camera, relying on a finely trained visual cortex formed over billions of years, I was not discovered. However, the white mask I wore was detected. We saw that my light-skinned partner was immediately spotted under the identical settings. Though this example focuses on facial recognition, computer vision can also be used to identify cancer or a person crossing the street. I'm less concerned with optimising computers to detect faces and more curious about how we train machines to look. The white mask protest is a starting point for broader discussions concerning prejudice in artificial intelligence and the people who can be hurt by these systems. Because of my experience with the coded gaze, I was particularly interested in computer vision systems for a variety of reasons. The study area dealing with the ability to recognize items such as faces was generally classified as "computer vision." I was interested in techniques to assist robots in perceiving and interpreting the world as a previous robotics hobbyist. Machines could use computer vision to recognize items or figure out how to navigate about an area, such as a Roomba vacuuming a living room while avoiding collisions with furniture. Not all computer vision tasks, such as detecting the borders of an image or creating a mosaic, require AI; but, when it came to systems evaluating human faces, AI was increasingly being deployed.

Between 2010 and 2016, there was a huge advance in the realm of artificial intelligence when I went from using my roommate's face to get Simon the robot to play peekaboo to showing a demo of putting on a white mask to have my face detected. While the old paradigm for programming computers was to provide specific instructions for a task, which can work at lightning speed for things like addition, subtraction, and sorting information, this approach failed when we pushed computers to do more complex tasks that might be considered a marker of intelligence beyond the ability to perform mathematical operations. Artificial intelligence, in my opinion, is the ongoing search to give computers the ability to perceive the world (that is, to make sense of visual, auditory, and other sensory inputs), to make judgments, to develop creative work, and to communicate with humans. And when I think about computers communicating with humans, I think of giving them the ability to read text or speech and then training them to reply convincingly. In the ideal case, this ongoing search for artificial intelligence can come together in a complex system such as a self-driving car. To traverse the world in real time and analyse visual information, the car needs sensory input that can be processed: That's another car, a tree, and a person. The car might be outfitted with various AI applications, such as speech recognition, so that it can "listen" for requests such as "Play 'Fear of the Water' by SYML." The vehicle may also offer turn-by-turn navigation. Even more challenging, the car may be in a situation where life is on the line, when one turn can save one life but end another. Responsibility comes with intelligence. Deriving meaning from complicated inputs when there are numerous possible interpretations makes artificial intelligence very difficult to achieve by explicitly writing code for every possible choice. The breakdown of rule-based expert systems, which were formerly popular in the field of AI, was an illustration of this challenge. Human specialists with considerable expertise in a specialised topic, such as diagnosing a medical ailment or a specific language group, such as Akan, inspired expert systems. Expert systems were developed with a knowledge base of explicit facts and relationships for a specific area, such as language translation. Linguists would meticulously strive to specify the rules of different languages to assist translation in order to gain knowledge of a translation system. However, the real world rarely adheres to all of the rules. When you need customer care to refund your order, spoken language and text chat do not strictly adhere to precise grammar. The IBM 701 computer translated simple Russian words into English in 1954, sparking widespread interest in machine translation. Dr. Dostert, one of the project's researchers, hailed the achievement in a press release as "a Kitty Hawk of electronic translation." The corporation was not bashful about seeking additional funding by putting their endeavour next to the Wright brothers' first successful flying machine demonstration. However, by 1966, when the Automatic Language Processing Advisory Committee (ALPAC) report was released, interest had waned. The National Science Foundation commissioned ALPAC to advise the agency, as well as the Department of Defense and the Central Intelligence Agency, on the possibility for "mechanical translation of foreign languages." The analysis demonstrated that current procedures were not up to the level of quality supplied by human translators and advocated investing in strategies to help human translators become more efficient as research continued. The ALPAC report revealed that the hoped-for skills, such as human language mastery, were only just beginning to be explored in the then-nascent field of natural language processing (NLP); work on this subject continues in NLP to this day.

IN 1956, AT THE FAMOUS Dartmouth Summer Research Project, where the term "artificial intelligence" was coined, researchers proposed that in two months, ten men could make significant progress in at least one of the areas outlined in their proposal, including "how to make machines use language." However, a decade later, the ALPAC study found slow development. An AI winter followed, with research funding dwindling and graduate students instructed to pursue more promising areas of study. A new approach to the continuous search for artificial intelligence was required. Rather than coding explicit instructions for every potential option or pattern and failing, a more robust technique for machines to see and communicate with the world evolved. A baby is not born with the ability to navigate the environment, communicate, or make sound judgments. The learning process takes place through observation and imitation. Using this process as a model, machine learning evolved as one of the primary artificial intelligence approaches in the early twenty-first century. Instead of teaching machines all the rules explicitly, what if we could train them to learn from examples? Machine learning is a less strict approach to artificial intelligence than rule-based expert systems. Do you want a computer to recognize your face? Rather than attempting to write code to specify every possible way a face could appear in an image, supply a dataset of photos including instances of faces. In the field of computer vision, visual training data can be used to train a machine to detect a variety of items, such as cats, chihuahuas, cupcakes, malignant cell cultures, combatants, and civilians. However, we must keep in mind that these systems do not always get it right. When machine learning systems mix together combatants and civilians instead of cupcakes and chihuahuas, the results are drastically different. One of the main issues with artificial intelligence is that the techniques being developed can be tuned for a wide range of applications, from benign to lethal. Because AI can be used in a variety of scenarios ranging from cupcakes to warriors, the examples of how the technology is used impact public perception of what is achievable as well as potential threats. When companies like Boston Dynamics demonstrate its autonomous dog-like quadruped robots doing something charming, such as dancing, they conceal the ways these systems may be utilised in military or law enforcement operations. To raise awareness about algorithmic bias, I needed to choose an app that could show people the dangers of AI. Although the concept of using machine learning in the pursuit of artificial intelligence has been present since the mid-twentieth century, a few critical components have been offered in the twenty-first century. Machines, unlike humans, frequently require a large number of examples to learn. A machine learning-based object detection model in computer vision may rely on millions of pictures. Access to such a massive number of photographs was largely impracticable prior to the advent of the internet. Sites for sharing photographs with tags, such as Flickr, offered the requisite treasure mine of labelled data. The ability to store vast volumes of data and process that data fast was also required. Increased computer power and storage capacity at a lower cost aided in the viability and adoption of mobile devices. As cellphones became more popular, more information was created and shared on the internet. The founders of social media platforms such as Facebook and Twitter, as well as the developers of mobile operating systems such as Google's Android, were able to accumulate vast amounts of valuable user data. Many of us were unknowingly accelerating the advancement of AI. Data availability improvements and improved computer power were critical enablers. But there was one more thing we needed. How can a machine be taught to learn from data? To accomplish this achievement, AI researchers once again looked to the brain for inspiration. Our brains are made up of neurons that are intricately linked together. Certain connections between our neurons increase as we learn, while others diminish. A single neuron cannot perform a difficult task like face recognition, but by working together, little components may perform larger tasks. Researchers developed artificial neural networks based on this concept. Instead of neurons and synapses, the artificial neural network is made up of nodes that are connected in a web of layers. Neurons inspired the nodes, and synapses inspired the links. Keep in mind that just because machine learning is inspired by some aspects of the biological brain does not imply that we are developing sentient or conscious machines. We are more than our biology as people. Consider the neural network to be a pattern recognizer. These networks can have a variety of topologies depending on how the nodes are connected to one another and how many layers are present. Nodes can alternatively be compared to marshmallows that can be joined with toothpicks. The placement of marshmallows and toothpicks determines the network's design. You select alternative architectures based on your objectives. Are you building a multi-level bridge or a simple V shape? Weights define the strength of the connections between linked nodes. Think of a strong link between two marshmallows as a thicker toothpick or a heavier weight. The stronger the bond, the greater the weight. When a neural network is originally created, the weights are not set up to respond to a specific pattern, such as a face. A neural network must be trained to respond to a specific type of pattern in order to be useful. A neural network's training procedure strengthens some connections while weakening others so that the trained neural network model can recognize a pattern. To generate machine learning models, which are neural networks built to detect a given pattern, researchers have devised many types of training approaches. In general, machine learning components include training data, testing data, a neural network to set up, and a learning algorithm to grow the neural network's expertise. Remember that an algorithm is a set of instructions used to achieve a given result. A learning method for a neural network's purpose is to optimise the weights between the nodes in order to recognize a pattern. In the example of detecting an object in an image, such as a car, the neural network is exposed to many training photos including a car, and the weights are modified several times until the model can reliably detect cars in images to which it has not previously been exposed. Natural language processing, like computer vision, has evolved as a result of machine learning. Some of the 1960s' unattainable goals, such as machine translation from one language to another, are now achievable for human languages that are available in vast numbers online. Large language models (LLMs), which enable chatbots, are also trained to recognize patterns. Many LLMs are trained using material from the internet, which means they consume massive amounts of knowledge from a large fraction of what has been made public online. Newspaper articles, scientific papers, standardised test questions and answers, and the entirety of Wikipedia are just a few examples of sources that can make somebody appear incredibly knowledgeable. (Imagine taking a test while having access to all of the example questions and correct answers that have been put online, and then providing comparable responses. I'm not saying you're not smart, or that you don't have an advantage, but I'd be less pleased.) These systems consume not only credible content, but also harmful stuff from online forums, hate speech on social media, and other sources. LLM students learn the good, terrible, and ugly. LLMs take a step beyond image classifiers. Instead than being taught to recognize a pattern like a face, kids are taught to recognize linguistic patterns and then recreate such patterns convincingly when prompted. So, if you ask an LLM, "What indigenous languages are missing on the internet?" you may expect a meaningful and grammatically correct response. However, the answer may be inadequate because some missing languages may never have been identified on the internet at all. The internet does not contain all of human knowledge. The training data gives the neural network experience that it can use to new data and prompts. However, inexperience has consequences. One important difficulty with neural networks is that computer scientists do not always understand why some weights are reinforced while others are lowered during the training process. As a result, present methodologies do not allow us to fully describe how a neural network detects a pattern such as a face or responds to a command. Because AI systems contain inexplicable components, the term "black box" may be used to characterise them. While it is true that some aspects of the process are difficult to explain, we must nonetheless carefully evaluate the AI systems that are being produced. When it comes to recognizing the hazards posed by an AI system, having access to the training data is critical. We can't tell if ethical methods were employed unless we know where the data came from, who collected it, and how it was arranged. Was the information collected with consent? What were the working conditions and compensation for the data processors? These inquiries extend beyond the technical. When I first started learning about neural networks, I was curious about how well they functioned in a specific context. As a computer scientist, I was taught to prioritise the technological over the ethical. My awareness of the social and environmental ramifications of AI emerged barely more than a decade after I first learnt to code. Returning to the technical, after a system has been trained on a set of data, we evaluate how effectively the neural network responds to the patterns it has been trained for. Our comprehension of a neural network's performance is strongly reliant on the data we use to evaluate it. The original neural networks were quite rudimentary, with only a few layers. As computational power expanded, researchers were able to build more complicated networks with many extra layers, giving rise to deep learning. Deep learning is a subset of machine learning that employs multilayered pattern recognizers inspired by the neural connections of the brain. Consider a large number of marshmallows and toothpicks in this example. There could be billions of parameters in the systems used to construct generative AI products that can generate visuals from text such as "an astronaut riding a horse in space." There can be trillions of parameters in LLMs. Weights can be used to indicate how strongly distinct components of the design are coupled via parameters. Machine learning is simply one method for computers to make decisions or develop new information based on suggestions. There is more to the story, but this high-level summary provides a starting point for understanding how some of the most extensively used artificial intelligence systems become vulnerable to negative discrimination and poisonous outputs. Decisions are not impartial just because they are made by a computer examining data. Neural does not imply neutral. Some easy decision-making systems adhere to stated restrictions, such as not allowing anyone under the age of sixteen access to content or a certain score on a risk assessment declaring you ineligible for credit. Whatever approach is taken, if an automated judgement affects your opportunities and liberties, you must have a voice and a say in whether and how technology is employed. I use the term "coded gaze" in my work to remind myself that the machines we develop reflect the goals, preferences, and even prejudices of individuals with the authority to define technology. The coded gaze does not have to be obvious in order to oppress. It is woven into the fabric of society, just like systematic forms of oppression such as patriarchy and racial supremacy. people who have had power in the past continue to pass that power on to people who are most like them if no one intervenes. This does not have to be done on purpose to have a bad effect. The objective at hand was to see whether I could locate convincing evidence of the coded gaze at work.

CHAPTER 6
FACIAL RECOGNITION TECHNOLOGIES

People began writing to me about their experiences with facial recognition after I made my TED.com debut. One woman told me about being contacted by casino security personnel who accosted her for allegedly being a sex worker while on vacation in Las Vegas. The casino's camera security systems had apparently incorrectly identified her as someone else. I also received a handwritten letter from an inmate appealing to me to look into their case because they felt they were imprisoned because of a bogus face recognition match. These experiences, as well as the flood of comments concerning real-world interactions with the coded gaze, terrified and overwhelmed me. With these and other direct accounts of AI failures, the Algorithmic Justice League began to feel more like a developing movement than a graduate school project. With the influx of testimonials, it was evident that flawed technical systems had already contributed to disproportionate scrutiny, suspicion, and, in the instance of the convict who wrote to me, jail time. So I began classifying these machine learning failure scenarios. I was astonished to learn that machine learning could have an impact on my romantic life. I attempted to join a dating app that looked to employ AI on uploaded photographs before granting access. I returned to my research after the algorithm failed to locate a face on my first two attempts to upload a profile photo. I'd already read about how failing machine learning may rob you of your liberty. However, it was evident to me that machine failures do not just refer to situations of misidentification, detection failures, or other system flaws. Machine decisions can potentially be used in ways that violate our expectations of fairness. A Harvard University investigation discovered price disparities in the Princeton Review's online SAT tutoring program. Researchers discovered that rates for the internet service varied by zip code after evaluating thirty-three thousand zip codes. According to a ProPublica analysis, customers in areas with a high proportion of Asian inhabitants were 1.8 times more likely to pay higher costs for online tutoring regardless of income. I also remembered the EyeSee mannequin, which was starting to appear in stores around the country. These mannequins, created by the Italian company Almax SpA, were outfitted with a camera and coupled with software that silently recognized shoppers' faces and estimated their age, gender, and ethnicity. Unlike the widely visible security cameras located on the walls of department stores, these cameras were disguised in plain sight, surreptitiously filming clients at eye level. What would businesses do with the demographic data gathered by these mannequins? Women have previously suffered a "pink tax," which means paying more for things like pens and razors that are pink rather than blue or black. Systems developed to measure demographics could use that information in business contexts to affect which customers received and which did not receive particular promotions. My objective now was to determine whether the failures I had experienced or heard about were isolated incidents or indicative of something more widespread. I decided to concentrate my efforts on AI systems applied to human faces. A heated debate is raging over what to designate AI systems that study human looks. Because

AI systems can scan your face for a variety of functions, different technical words are used for each. Researchers, marketers, journalists, and policymakers can all use similar-sounding terminology to represent distinct things, which can lead to misunderstanding. Even researchers and companies involved in the development of these systems do not always agree on terminology. When I encounter the term "facial recognition" in a paper or on a technology website, I attempt to figure out how it's defined—if it's defined at all. The Federal Trade Commission issued a report in 2012 stating that the phrase "facial recognition" was used generically to refer to any technique used to extract data from facial photographs. The term "facial recognition technologies" was used as a catch-all phrase throughout the report. I use this expression because it implies that machines can do a wide range of face-related jobs. However, being precise with terminology is more than just an academic exercise. The ability to define terminology has a significant impact on the reach and efficacy of legislation and regulation. Companies may also avoid terms that generate a lot of public scrutiny and backlash. Instead of mentioning a system that uses facial recognition, a corporation may use the phrase "face matching" to avoid criticism. I describe the various types of tasks performed by facial recognition technologies as investigations of three fundamental topics to aid increased understanding: Is there a face here? What kind of expression is this? Have I seen this expression before?

Some companies and researchers claim that their algorithms can identify a person's sexual orientation, political affiliation, IQ, or chance of committing a crime merely only on their facial traits. I recall my surprise when I came across a 2017 study in which the authors used photos of over eighteen hundred people to construct a classifier to predict criminality based on a face image. I was particularly concerned when I read in The Economist in September 2017 about Stanford academics who created classifiers to determine someone's sexual orientation based just on a photograph of their face. One of the researchers indicated in the article that with the correct dataset, they could "spot other intimate traits, such as IQ or political views." Predicting someone's psychological mood, identity, or future conduct solely only on visual traits is untrustworthy, but the impact can still be significant. Being called a criminal or homosexual might result in negative prejudice and, in extreme cases, death. The International Lesbian, Gay, Bisexual, Trans, and Intersex Association issued a report in December 2020 stating that 67 UN member states ban consenting same-sex sexual conduct, with six imposing the death penalty. Labels matter, thus we must be cautious of any organisation or researcher who claims to be able to predict psychological states, innate skills, or future behaviours using external attributes.

"Have I seen this face before?" is the inquiry that researchers classify as "facial recognition" as used by industry specialists. Biometrics professionals do not use the phrase "facial recognition" to refer to any type of data that may be extracted from a face. Instead, this use of facial recognition is centred on a person's unique identity. In terms of technology, there are two forms of facial recognition. One method is facial recognition, often known as one-to-one matching. The machine is answering the question: Does the face presented match the face expected? This is the task that is carried out when you unlock your phone with your face. The other sort of facial recognition that receives the greatest public attention is facial identification, often known as one-to-many matching. This is the process by which an image of your face—which might come from anywhere, from a snapshot you submit to social media to your look on a security camera—is compared to a database of probable matches. The database may be stored by a corporation such as Meta, the owner of Facebook, which has a large collection of photos of people's faces, or by a government agency such as the FBI, which permits police agencies to view those images. The possibilities for these one-to-many facial recognition systems are extensive, and are only limited by the ingenuity and resources of those with the authority to use them. Rite Aid, for example, added security cameras with facial recognition capabilities to verify faces against a database of previous shoplifters. Facial recognition technologies were being offered to law enforcement organisations in both the UK and the US. Big Brother Watch, a civil liberties organisation, published a study in 2018 claiming that the United Kingdom's Metropolitan Police Department has tested face recognition algorithms that incorrectly paired innocent members of the public with criminal suspects more than 98 percent of the time. South Wales Police performed marginally better, with 91 percent of false matches. During the procedure, 2,451 people's faces were unintentionally scanned by the department and stored for a year. The sooner I could conduct trials, the sooner I could collect evidence to assist organisations such as Big Brother Watch in preventing the negative use of facial recognition technologies. When facial recognition works properly, businesses and governments have sophisticated surveillance technologies at their disposal that can be used for social control and exclusion. When facial recognition fails, you may find yourself under investigation for a crime you did not commit, or confronted by security officers who have "digital evidence" that you resemble a thief, or misidentified as a prostitute in an area where sex work is prohibited. In any case, the stakes are great. Here are some more examples: Failures in facial recognition can hamper your capacity to receive crucial papers when used to access services such as renewing a government passport. When transportation security uses it, you may be tagged as a terrorist suspect, or you may find yourself unable to board a train that uses the face to pay or verify passengers' identities.

Now that you understand the distinctions between face verification (one-to-one matching) and facial identification (one-to-many matching), you can see why the word "facial recognition" needs to be defined when discussing policy. If we created a legislation defining facial recognition as simply one-to-one matching, it would not cover cases of facial identification being used for mass monitoring, such as during a protest or in a department store. If face recognition is limited to one-to-many matching, the law does not apply to circumstances in which an asylum seeker or elderly citizen attempts to receive government services using facial verification. If we return to the wide 2012 Federal Trade Commission definition of facial recognition, which includes any technology that analyses data from a face, the law becomes more protective. Gender classification, race classification, and age estimation are all examples of broad definitions. Such a rule would apply not only to circumstances in which your exact identity is captured, but also to cases in which your demographic or physical characteristics are obtained from your face and then exploited to violate your civil rights.

Because it would violate Title VII of the Civil Rights Act in the United States, a business could not implement a method that systematically screened out job seekers based on their race from facial data associated with an online profile link. Title VII prohibits employers from discriminating against candidates based on their race, gender, or colour, among other factors. This is where facial detection comes into play. If a company used an AI system to differentiate between real and fake job applicants by looking up face images of the people, and the face detection model it used failed on darker-skinned individuals, it would systematically conclude that dark-skinned applicants were fake, putting them at a disadvantage. This conduct could place the corporation in violation of Title VII. After a complaint from the Electronic Privacy Information Center (EPIC) and an audit from O'Neil Risk Consulting & Algorithmic Auditing (ORCAA), HireVue, a company that claimed to utilise AI to evaluate video of a candidate to estimate problem-solving ability, eventually removed the feature. Other organisations, however, use AI algorithms to evaluate videos and faces as part of the interview process. Aside from jobs, there are concerns with schooling. When remote learning became necessary due to the COVID-19 pandemic, e-proctoring enterprises gained traction. To combat cheating, schools used e-proctoring techniques to monitor distant students while they took tests. These companies received complaints from students with dark skin who had to put up intricate lighting contraptions to be seen, couldn't be authenticated to log in, or were marked as cheating. When the system no longer detects a face, the cheating flag appears. However, there are technical reasons why a face may not be spotted that are unrelated to cheating and instead signal a failure of the AI system. After facing distant test conditions that required her to shine a light on her face to take her exams, Dutch student Robin Pocornie filed a complaint with the Netherlands Institute for Human Rights. Similar complaints were not filed by white pupils. The institute looked into the allegation and issued an interim ruling in her favour, concluding that the software utilised by her university, VU Amsterdam, discriminates against Black students.[15] These technologies can also disadvantage those with disabilities, as the Center for Democracy and Technology discovered in a study of e-proctoring tools: Students with attention deficit disorder (ADD) who get up and pace around the room may be identified by AI video analysis. Students with Tourette's syndrome who have movement tics, students with cerebral palsy who have involuntary spasms, or autistic students who flap or rock could be flagged. It could detect dyslexic students who read questions aloud or blind students who use screen-reader software that speaks aloud. It could identify students with Crohn's disease or irritable bowel syndrome who need to leave the classroom frequently to use the restroom. It could detect blind or autistic students with unusual eye movements. Because all of these movements and responses are normal aspects of many different types of disability, algorithmic virtual proctoring software cannot accommodate impaired students. The goal is to identify and highlight abnormal movement, behaviour, or communication; disabled persons will, by definition, move, behave, and communicate abnormally. When businesses force employees to conform to a restrictive notion of acceptable behaviour encoded in a machine learning model, they perpetuate negative patterns of exclusion and distrust. I had my work cut out for me when it came to commencing my research—I wanted to direct my work so that it would be put to good use and have some impact in the world even before I fully grasped the damages I suspected and the harms to come. I entered the domain of computer vision research because facial identification was already being employed by law enforcement, and my experience with face detection failure was part of what inspired me to start researching in the first place. However, given the wide range of facial recognition technologies available—and the numerous applications for which they are already being used—I recognized I needed to focus my efforts and better grasp what was already known about the accuracy of these systems.

CHAPTER 7
POWER SHADOWS

The hard fun started in earnest. Creating a system that can detect, classify, or recognize a face is only half the battle. To do the training, you acquire a dataset of faces. The other battleground is determining how effectively that system works. The conventional procedure for researchers is to choose a benchmark, which is a dataset used as the baseline against which newly built systems can be assessed. And, in any given research group, there is usually agreement among researchers on which benchmarks are particularly rigorous. For example, in the early days of developing one-to-one facial recognition systems that could later be used to unlock devices such as smartphones, a dataset known as Labelled Faces in the Wild (LFW)—a collection of over thirteen thousand images of nearly fifty-eight hundred people—became the gold standard benchmark.One of the significant shortcomings of previous benchmarks was that the majority of the photographs in these datasets were taken in controlled situations. Consider what occurs when you pose for a professional portrait in front of a camera: The lighting is perfect, the camera is focused directly at you, and the photographer directs your stance to catch your face precisely. Early facial recognition systems performed well on these standards, but their performance dropped when subjected to real-world settings. Labelled Faces in the Wild was a significant step forward since it was made up of photographs acquired "in the wild"—that is, images not captured in a studio—and so forced academics to develop algorithms that would theoretically perform better in the real world.

As researchers developed new approaches for one-to-one facial recognition, their colleagues would assess the state of the art based on how well it performed against LFW. For a period, the accuracy remained below 80%. Then, in 2014, a huge breakthrough occurred when Facebook researchers published a paper titled "DeepFace" that reported 97.35 percent performance on the gold standard LFW benchmark, breaking the plateau. The artificial intelligence community was ecstatic because it demonstrated the possibilities of employing deep learning for facial recognition. It's no coincidence that Facebook was able to do significant facial recognition research:

Users on its social networking platform had submitted personal photographs with faces, and many of those images had been tagged to other Facebook users; these networks created a massive dataset for the corporation to study for research purposes. Reporters were enthusiastic about the "DeepFace" study, pushing it up for the general public with headlines like "Facebook's DeepFace Project Nears Human Accuracy in Identifying Faces." Reading this report and others that quickly followed, I could see why there was growing trust in facial recognition algorithms. With research from influential companies like Facebook, Google, and Microsoft, as well as research from some of the world's best computer vision labs, demonstrating high accuracy rates on the gold standard, it's no surprise that people assumed the technology was mature enough to use in the real world. Government reports bolstered this sense of hope. The National Institute of Standards and Technology (NIST), for example, set criteria for a variety of biometric technology such as fingerprints and faces. Biometric technology companies that created systems for law enforcement submitted them to NIST for testing. NIST benchmarks included tasks such as gender categorization and facial identification in addition to facial verification. From 2010 to 2014, government tests revealed an overall improvement in the performance of facial identification systems. These promising results enhanced researchers' confidence in the use of facial recognition in the actual world.

However, just because a standard is embraced and becomes the norm does not mean it should be ignored. Despite the advancements I read about, my own experience coding while wearing a white mask made me cautious. At the very least, I wanted to go deeper into the specifics. In the first place, how precious were these criteria in the first place—what standards were they held up to before researchers judged their worth to the research community? I discovered a minimal study that investigated the demographics of who was included in databases like LFW. This omission could be explained in part by the fact that these photographs were collected from the internet for convenience. Labelling and analysing datasets requires time and resources as well. As a result, it was standard practice to collect a huge dataset, such as a collection of images featuring human faces, and merely know that the dataset comprised X number of faces without knowing the actual demographic breakdown of the faces. If I did come across research on the demographic mix of databases, the picture was clear. Hu Han and Anil Jain investigated the demographic composition of LFW in 2014, discovering that the image database contains 77.5 percent male-labelled faces and 83.5 percent white-labelled faces. It was discovered that the gold standard for facial recognition was severely distorted. I began referring to these as "pale male datasets."

The Han and Jain paper prompted me to examine other benchmarks more closely. Another public face collection that included photographs of celebrities and prominent personalities was IMDB-Wiki. It made sense for benchmarks like IMDB-Wiki to rely on photographs of famous people: Not only are there a wealth of photographs available online, but they can also be easily labelled with identifying information, which is useful when teaching robots to recognize faces. As a result, these records represented the demographic makeup of Hollywood rather than the rest of the population, and were biassed primarily toward the young, white, and male. I then focused on the datasets coming out of NIST, which has two types of datasets: sequestered data used to test systems internally and public datasets released to aid progress research in the field. NIST had released a public dataset of faces named IJB-A at the time I was working on my MIT master's thesis. The goal of this dataset was to give more diversity—specifically, regional diversity—while also overcoming another issue with benchmark development: face detection failure. Instead of having a human search for photos one by one and check the image for a face to automatically collect photos of images online, researchers built code that used search engines to do image searches. Because the researchers only wanted photographs with faces and not all other types of images found on the internet, they would frequently include code for automatic face detection to filter the images. As a result, the composition of a dataset obtained using this method is greatly dependent on the quality of the face detection code utilised. While researchers were able to acquire vast volumes of face data without obtaining authorization, they were missing useful data that includes faces missed by the face detector. I expanded my study by conducting an intersectional analysis based on the work of Kimberlé Crenshaw, a famous legal scholar. Her groundbreaking work on antidiscrimination law in the United States exposed the limitations of analysing discrimination cases using a single-axis analysis such as gender or race. She demonstrated that persons who faced various forms of intersecting discrimination, such as women of colour, were being disregarded by the way the laws were worded. There could be redress if you were discriminated against because you were a woman, Asian, or Black, but the law didn't enable you to allege discrimination on two fronts. For example, the Equal Employment Opportunity Commission (EEOC) has a four-fifths rule that states that if you can establish that the minority group is receiving less than 80% of similar opportunities as opposed to the majority group, you have a basis for a lawsuit. The problem for a Black woman would be that the numbers in aggregate for all women or all Black people at a company might be legal, and as long as white women and Black men were getting opportunities, there was no basis to claim gender or race discrimination at the company. However, if Black women or Asian women were denied those opportunities, they had no legal basis to seek redress because the employer might claim that they employed women and Black people or Asian people. However, as writer and activist Audre Lorde points out, individuals do not live single-issue lives. From my vantage point, it looked that the machine learning community has yet to implement these anti-discrimination scholarship discoveries. The emphasis on benchmark accuracy was frequently limited to one metric: total performance. What would it look like if we started to separate performance across different axes of analysis? What would we learn about a system's capabilities and limitations? How far would we go if we looked at which groups were included and, more importantly, which groups were excluded?

Meeting Crenshaw's intersectionality work—in a seemingly unrelated field to mine—opened the door to asking deeper questions about my study and about AI in general. My undergraduate computer science education had prepared me to look under the hood of machine learning systems, and my personal experiences with the coded gaze piqued my interest, but it was the scholarship of Black women scholars that I encountered in graduate school that provided me with the language to articulate what I was seeing in AI. This concept of intersectionality—or assessing across various axes of identity—was applied to my review of the NIST benchmark. The intersectional analysis was eye-opening. When I examined the composition of the government dataset not just by gender or skin type individually, but also by the intersections of many parameters, I discovered that lighter-skinned males accounted for 59.4 percent of the total benchmark, while women of colour accounted for only 4.4 percent. Even if a system fails on all women of colour in the sample, it can attain an overall accuracy rate of 95.6 percent and be considered adequate for the actual world. Beyond faces, deep learning techniques were being used to train algorithms to identify skin cancer or pedestrians for use in self-driving cars. If those datasets were likewise skewed, AI cancer detectors might not perform well for groups of persons who were underrepresented in the dataset. It would imply that automated vehicles would be more prone to collide with certain groups of individuals than others. I began to comprehend why what I was reading in study papers and what I was feeling contradicted each other. Because the benchmarks lacked representation, they hid possible bias. The gold standards were pyrite, or fool's gold, with sparkling accuracy in their numbers but not a structure reflective of all people. Nonetheless, experts accepted them as the status quo. One significant takeaway for me was to always question so-called gold standards. Standards employed in AI may appear to be off-limits for questioning when we presume the professionals have done a thorough job, just as the standard Shirley cards used for calibrating film-based photography may appear impartial or untouchable. This is not always the case, especially when the experts do not accurately represent the rest of society. But design is not fate. I realised I had to make an attempt to reform the system.

When using machine learning to detect hate speech, diagnose medical conditions, or inform hiring decisions, we must keep in mind that the past lives in our data. In the instance of hiring, Amazon discovered this lesson when it developed a model for screening resumes. The model was trained using data from previous successful employees who were chosen by humans, so human decision-makers' earlier decisions became the basis for training the system. Internal tests indicated that the model was rejecting résumés including the word "women" or colleges affiliated with women. The system has discovered that previous successful candidates were mostly men.

Previous employment practices and decades of denying women the opportunity to study, along with the difficulties encountered while enrolled in higher school, made it exceptionally difficult to break into male-dominated sectors. It filtered out résumés that indicated an applicant was a woman based on the data the algorithm was trained on. This was a result of previous human decisions that favoured men. The initial approach was not used by Amazon since the engineers were unable to remove the gender bias. Stopping is a viable and necessary option. I discovered data that was not typical of society in the face databases I analysed. The Amazon recruiting approach exemplifies what happens when data accurately reflects societal expectations. Power shadows were mirrored in their model. When a society's biases or systemic exclusion are mirrored in data, power shadows are cast. Seeing the significant skews toward lighter-skinned individuals and men in the face datasets compelled me to investigate why these biases occurred. How did these datasets come to be collected in the first place? Answers began to appear when I used the government standard as a starting point. To address privacy concerns, the researchers chose to focus on prominent individuals who, by virtue of their jobs in society, frequently as public workers, have a level of visibility that makes information about their demographic features public knowledge. While utilising public figures could potentially alleviate certain privacy problems, the decision itself was fraught with power dynamics. Who holds political power? It is unsurprising that men have historically held political power around the world, and we continue to witness patriarchy at work when it comes to leadership and decision-making. At the time I was conducting my research, UN Women published a chart illustrating the gender disparity in women's representation in parliaments. According to this data, men made up 76.7 percent of parliament members on average. As a result, while generating a dataset based on parliament members, the patriarchy already casts a shadow. While this could partially explain the male tilt, I also wanted to learn more about the disproportionate number of lighter-skinned people. According to Nina Jablonski's research on skin distribution around the world, the majority of the world's populations have skin that falls on the darker end of most skin classification scales. Returning to the government IJB-A dataset, which was designed to have the greatest geographic diversity of any face dataset, how did it manage to have more than 80% lighter-skinned individuals?

When we examine who wields power around the world, we can see the impact of colonialism and colorism, which stem from the power shadow of white supremacy. Formerly colonised states that gained independence retained the colonial authority system. White immigrants and their descendants were frequently lighter than indigenous peoples or darker African enslaved people imported into conquered countries. This impact became clear to me when I began studying the composition of parliaments around the world. Despite the fact that South Africa's population is 80.8 percent Black, 8.7 percent coloured, and 2.6 percent Asian, approximately 20% of legislators are white. Leaving a colonial past behind does not decolonize the psyche. White supremacy, like the white gaze, dictates who is worthy of attention and what is considered beautiful or desirable as a cultural instrument. Colorism is the forgotten stepchild of white supremacy. Colorism works by attaching high social worth and economic standing to people depending on the colour of their skin, so that even if two people are of the same race, the person with lighter skin is considered better. This is evident in Hollywood and Bollywood. With its diverse skin tones, India has an entertainment and beauty business that promotes light-skinned actors and actresses. Women are rated on their beauty, and the beauty standard is based on proximity to fair skin. In countries influenced by white supremacy, lighter complexion is likewise correlated with higher IQ. Hollywood has historically favoured white actors, and when it began to broaden significantly, lead roles for different cast members likewise favoured the lighter complexion. This is not to argue that there were no famous or intellectual people with black skin during the time I was conducting this research. The point is that they were the exception rather than the rule. Returning to face datasets, we must consider how the photographs are collected. When a specific group, such as elected officials, is chosen as a target dataset, the images obtained are based on videos and photographs of the persons. Again, we can see the growing shadow of white supremacy. Which lawmakers are more likely to have photos and videos online? If you require at least 10 photos or video clips to be included in the dataset, the representatives who receive greater media attention will have an edge. Even if you do not use automated methods such as face detection, which has been demonstrated to fail more frequently on darker-skinned faces, the availability of photographs based on media interest will still favour lighter-skinned people. Despite the objective of creating a more diversified dataset with representatives from all around the world, the government dataset was predominantly male and pale, inheriting the power shadows of patriarchy and white supremacy. These are not the only types of power shadows to be concerned about. Another type of power shadow that is frequently lurking in datasets, particularly those used for computer vision, is ableism, which favours able-bodied individuals. Few datasets for pedestrian tracking particularly contain individuals who use assistive aids. Power shadows reveal existing societal hierarchies based on race, gender, aptitude, and other factors, much as the past does in our data. Using convenient data collection methods to collect what is most popular and most accessible will mirror existing power systems. I could now understand how, despite all of the technical advancements brought about by the triumph of deep learning, I ended up coding in whiteface at MIT by delving into my study of facial recognition technology. Existing gold standards did not capture the entire sepia spectrum of humankind. Skewed gold standard benchmark datasets provide a misleading sense of universal progress based on evaluating the performance of facial recognition technology on a limited subset of humankind. Unaltered data collection systems that rely on prominent figures inherited power shadows, resulting in an overrepresentation of men and people with lighter skin. We must be conscious of power shadows in order to overcome them. We must also be deliberate in our approach to developing data-driven technology. The status quo falls well short of expectations. I would need to demonstrate novel approaches to benchmark dataset construction as well as more in-depth approaches to evaluate the performance of facial recognition technology. Could displaying my limits allow me to advocate for a new normal?

CHAPTER 8
CRAWLING THROUGH DATA

Early spring blossoms were trying to entice Cambridge out of its tough winter, and I was in my second year at MIT. As a result of changing my research focus in the fall of 2016, I only had a few months to perform my algorithmic bias tests and a few more to write a thesis about my findings and their implications. In the spring of 2017, despite being only twenty-seven years old, I didn't feel like time was on my side—there was so much to do. My experience coding in a white mask revealed an example of face detection failure, but I wanted my MIT research to go beyond detection to demonstrate yet another area in the study of the face that required attention. I concentrated my research on algorithms that predicted facial features such as gender, race, and age. Unlike ethnicity and age, which might be classified in a variety of ways, practically all gender classification systems at the time offered only two options: male and female. Though gender is not binary, the fact that most AI systems use only two gender possibilities makes focusing on binary gender classification a more simple decision. Nonetheless, I looked into other possibilities. More than two groups would be required for accurate race classification and age estimation. I experimented with having workers on Amazon Mechanical Turk (a platform that allows academics to post low-paying microtasks for crowdsourced workers to complete) categorise photographs from an existing face dataset with age, gender, and race labels. The identical faces would be shown to a number of turkers, and I would analyse the labels. When it came to determining age, having turkers predict a range rather than a single age gave more consistent results. When it came to estimating race, I first used U.S. Census categories and left an "other" category open. That category's results supplied the most information. It became evident that the Census categories were inadequate for dealing with people perceived as South Asian, Southeast Asian, Middle Eastern, or mixed ethnicity by tourists. (Because the faces revealed were of public figures, the turkers had access to more information than just the image shown.) Gender was the most consistent of the three categories to label, tipping the scales in favour of gender classification. These investigations demonstrate how deeply humans are involved in the development of automated systems. Examining the many classifications given to the same face by Turks revealed the amount of guesswork that went into attempting to categorise perceived race. Following the turkers' studies, I began using "perceived race" instead of "race" when discussing classification. Setting up microtasks provided me power and elevated my viewpoints. It was my human option to select classification categories into which the turkers were subsequently forced to fit. My own classification categories were influenced by how others had previously classified persons. As a beginning point, I looked to existing systems, such as the U.S. Census race categories, which have evolved throughout time and reflect the social, political, and economic context of the day. For example, before 2000, the United States Census, which began in 1790, did not enable people to categorise themselves into several racial groupings. It was in 1960 that census takers first had the ability to self-identify how they fit within the available possibilities. The categories changed as well, with enslaved people becoming "colored," then "Black," and finally "Negro." In the 2020 census, the phrase "African American" was first used. None of this categorization felt precise, and, like the census classifications, my options were not neutral. They were influenced by the time period and those in positions of authority.I still had to deal with the concept of race after electing to focus on gender categorization for the purpose of the technical simplicity of binary classification. My face not being noticed in the first place, I reasoned, had more to do with my dark complexion than with my gender. I didn't want to experiment with gender classification just for the purpose of it. I was curious to examine if these systems affected the performance of diverse groups of people. I needed to include more than gender categories in my research, so I embarked on an unexpected journey into the field of ethnic enumeration. I discovered that the rationale for categorising people by race and ethnicity varied over the world, as did the use of the terms race, ethnicity, or colour to define the categorization. In South Africa, for example, racial classifications were purposefully and publicly connected to economic, social, and political interactions in order to maintain apartheid. Being classed as white, coloured, or black had a significant impact on an individual's life chances.

When I was in Cape Town, South Africa, for a tech conference in 2019, I went to the "Classification Building," where people could have their hair and even their most private areas checked to identify race. Sandra Liang, who was born to white Afrikaans parents yet presents in a way that classifies her as coloured, is an example of how race is manufactured. It was thus feasible for white parents to have a coloured daughter who was shunned by the white community and eventually found safety in a township. In areas like Canada, the term "visible minority" is used, which recognizes that external appearance is what is utilised to generate racial judgments with substantial societal repercussions. In Canada, as in the United Kingdom and the United States, racial categorization is used by the government to better understand where resources should be allocated and to protect minority groups or individuals who may encounter discrimination. In the instance of the United States, I saw a discrepancy between this declared purpose and the current census classification, which placed Middle Easterners in the category of white. Individuals considered as white and those perceived as Middle Eastern were treated and discriminated against differently, particularly after the September 11th World Trade Center attack. This is far from the only inconsistency to be discovered. I was also astonished to learn of Europe's diverse ethnic groupings, as I had been trained to apply the broad designation of white to those having European ancestors. I discovered that, in European countries such as France and Germany, foregoing ethnic enumeration in order to construct a national identity—despite a vast range of ethnicities with their own cultural norms and, in certain cases, method of speaking a shared language—was a conscious act. Reading this reminded me of a trip I did to Scotland with my Taiwanese buddy Alan, who introduced me to the diverse ethnic people in and around China. I told him that Ghana had over forty indigenous languages and a similar number of tribal groups, and that my mother had a pretty good eye for differentiating tribal membership, at least from my perspective. It also reminded me of my Fulbright scholarship in Zambia, where residents frequently questioned my tribal identity, presuming I was from the region. My classmates in Zambia also noticed that I have a West African smile. I had no idea there was such a thing until I ran a Google search, which revealed to their surprise that I did indeed have what they referred to as a West

African smile. Alan and I were walking behind two women who were discussing a new research that claimed there were substantial DNA distinctions between Scotsmen and Englishmen. Alan, whose girlfriend was a Frenchman, and I also discussed how amused we were to observe French and English hostility as we traversed Oxford University on our Rhodes Scholarships. To us, they all appeared "white," just as Alan appeared "Asian," and depending on where I was in the world, I appeared "Black," or for those with more expertise with "Black" faces, I appeared "West African." Nobody ever guessed I was a hybrid of the Ashanti and Dagua tribes. Race and ethnic classification are influenced by a mix of national techniques to ethnic enumeration, regional specialisation, and outward appearance. Living in different parts of the world and between cultures taught me about how phenotypic views vary. Being Black made me part of the majority in Zambia and Ghana. My parents grew up in a time when race was not a major societal concern. It took some time after we came to the United States for them to associate negative experiences with race. If I was treated unfairly, they would not assume it was because of my colour, but would instead inquire about the circumstances. Because I grew up in Oxford, Mississippi, the context of Black people being minorities and stigmatised formed my racial consciousness. My primary school buddy Billy invited the white kids in our class to his birthday party but did not invite me, and I assumed it was because I was Black. But it's possible that he didn't like me, or that it was a combination of the two. When I went into a technical subject like computer science, I wanted to leave these memories behind. Initially, I assumed that my research would be heavily focused on technological concerns. Further investigation revealed that any technology involved in classifying people based on necessity will be impacted by subjective human choices. Because classification systems do not appear out of nowhere, the act itself is not neutral. This is what the term socio technical research means, which highlights the importance of studying technology designed to evaluate humans while also taking into account the social context and power dynamics at play. Despite these complications, some researchers attempted to develop machine learning models to guess race and/or ethnicity, frequently failing to distinguish between the two. Some investigations were almost comically rudimentary, using classifications like "white" and "nonwhite." Others attempted to borrow from existing classification systems, employing names such as "caucasoid" and "negroid," which have roots in eugenics and scientific racism. I even discovered a website called Ethnic Celebrities and developed a system that collected photographs of celebrities with a combination of race and ethnic description. I even found one of the most thorough ethnic classification systems from the Australian Bureau of Statistics, which lists over 270 different cultural and ethnic groups. Despite my efforts to create certain technical distinctions, my attempt to categorise celebrities by ethnicity failed, particularly when dealing with multiracial people. Then there was the difficulty of determining how those who identified as Hispanic should be classed. Hispanic is the only ethnicity group on the US Census that can be assigned to various race groupings (for example, "White, Hispanic" or "Black, Hispanic"). I came to NIST since I knew I wasn't the first to try to define racial classification for face datasets. They had fared no better. Some of their research employed "white" and "black" labels, whereas larger studies avoided racial categories in favour of focusing on nationality. However, as a predictor of performance on distinct populations, nationality fell short. Overall country-level performance did not reveal anything about racial or ethnic variations in nations with high racial and ethnic diversity, such as Brazil or the United States.

After a few weeks of attempting to untangle and arrange this shifting social construct of race, I tried another angle. In looking at gender classification, my goal was not to see if I could come up with a better race or ethnic categorization system, but to see if someone's appearance affected gender classification accuracy. Instead of looking at race, I decided to look for a more objective metric, which is when I began to focus on not only demographic factors like gender and race, but also phenotypic attributes, such as skin colour. Because face-based gender classification using images relied on imaging technology, and skin responds to light, focusing on skin tone seemed to be a more particular and objective approach to be more specific and objective. So I started looking at other ways people have classed skin. While I thought I was getting away from the complexities of race classification, I quickly discovered that the Felix von Luschan scale, used by anthropologists, was also being used in ways that promoted scientific racism. Along the way, I became interested in how dermatologists, not anthropologists, view skin. Dermatologists look at skin reaction to UV radiation—thus skin type—rather than just skin colour, which can vary when exposed to sunshine. Skin colour and skin type are linked but not the same thing. Tanning in the summer, for example, can affect your skin colour without changing your skin type. Focusing on skin type today, I discovered a more scientific scale known as the Fitzpatrick skin phototype scale. It included four categories when it was first devised in 1975 by Harvard scientist Thomas B. Fitzpatrick. The first three categories were various reactions to sunlight of skin that was commonly classed as white in the United States, and the fourth group was for everyone else (the majority of the globe). The fourth "nonwhite" group was increased to three more in the 1980s. It wasn't quite a balanced scale, but it was more scientifically based and less convoluted than the Felix von Luschan scale's 36 points. So I decided to employ phenotypic classification based on skin type for the dataset I needed for my research. But I was afraid of explicitly identifying strangers based on the colour of their skin. Looking at how machine learning models are formed, we can observe the impact of what Kate Crawford refers to as the "politics of classification." The ability to define classification systems is a capability in and of itself. Cultural, political, and economic variables influence choices, and while these classifications may not have to be founded on definite distinctions, they nonetheless have an impact on individual lives and social attitudes. Despite the power shadows inherent in classification systems, these systems are frequently unchallenged. Instead, they are used as abbreviations. Morgan Klaus Scheuerman and his colleagues have done extensive research on how gender classification systems contribute to erasure, reification of social constructions, and reinforcement of gender stereotypes. In my research, I had to cope with both realising the limitations of the classification systems we employ and appreciating the utility of those systems in detecting discrimination, unfairness, or inequitable treatment. Yes, the categorization systems were troublesome, but by employing them, I was able to demonstrate their limits as well as the limitations of the other systems I investigated. To deal with those constraints, it is critical to point out the assumptions underlying the categories that are being used, so that there is no universal acceptance that they are the ones that must be used or that they are without flaws. So, while acknowledging that gender isn't binary and that the Fitzpatrick scale, the most scientific and least racist skin type scale I found, was heavily skewed toward lighter skin, I chose two classification systems to demonstrate why we should question machine learning model classifications in the first place. This began for me with binary gender classification. Crawling classification algorithms and deciding on labels to employ are key components of the process, but these labels must still be applied to data. After navigating the jungle of classification methods, discovering the limitations of binary gender classification, and switching to skin type classification rather than race-based classification, the next challenge was to collect my own dataset. For researchers, using earlier work is the default strategy if it is possible. Before I started working on my own dataset, I investigated to see what datasets were already available for gender classification. I discovered the Adience dataset, which was created expressly for use with gender classification research investigations. Although there was a near gender balance in this dataset, with 48 percent male faces and 52 percent female faces, it was still overwhelmingly pale, with 86 percent lighter-skinned individuals. Because I was interested in how systems would perform on darker-skinned persons, this skew toward light complexion, even with a gender-focused dataset, barred me from using it for my research. After analysing other datasets, I was satisfied that establishing a new dataset would not be recreating the wheel. It's one thing to criticise other datasets and point out flaws in previous research; it's quite another to try to construct your own. My investigation into the generation of datasets utilising convenient methods revealed that previous approaches were deficient. Power shadows increased the likelihood that adopting automated or celebrity-based data collection methods would produce substantially biassed results. I had to devise a new strategy. The United Nations served as a good beginning point. According to a UN Women report on gender representation, men make up roughly 77 percent of legislators worldwide. I discovered a chart on the Inter-Parliamentary Union website that would be crucial to my dataset creation work. The graphic ranked each UN member country according to the proportion of women in parliament. Rwanda led the globe in female representation with 61 percent, which could be ascribed to systemic reforms in the law requiring gender parity in political representation. Other African countries in the top ten were Senegal and South Africa, which tied for ninth position with Finland at 42 percent. The high ranking of these African countries that had stronger representation of women in power than their global peers provided me with a starting point for locating publically available photographs of prominent people who were female and had a higher possibility of having skin type on the darker end of the Fitzpatrick scale. I would still need to look into the numbers because supposition is not fact.

In the top 10, I discovered progressive Nordic countries whose egalitarian principles appeared to be partially mirrored when looking at the gender balance in parliament seats. It also helped that fair-skinned people on the opposite (lightest) end of the Fitzpatrick skin type scale were plentiful in Finland, Iceland, and Sweden. While there were countries in Central America that made the top ten, it appeared that their skin types would fall more in the middle range of the Fitzpatrick scale or into categories that were not well accounted for by the scale, so I decided to focus on people who would fall into the first two or last two categories of the scale. (I looked up where the United States placed out of curiosity. I spent some time scrolling. The United States ranked 100th out of 193 countries, at 19%.) After narrowing my options, I began collecting data on three high-ranking African parliaments and three high-ranking European parliaments. My curiosity got the best of me at this point, so I looked into the legislatures of several other countries, including Singapore, India, Brazil, and Haiti. My weekend adventures had progressed from passing photographs of my face through AI systems at tech companies to visiting government websites to visually scrutinise members of parliament. Despite their massive dark-skinned inhabitants, I was amazed at how light-skinned power appeared in Caribbean nations. And I found it fascinating to see African countries that I had been brainwashed to believe were lagging behind the rest of the globe in terms of gender representation leading the way. Other potential dataset explorations I had included looking at Olympic teams. The Olympics, like the UN, brought together people from all over the world, but I also had to consider the reality that elite athletes were not always representative of the general population in terms of skill, physical condition, or age. An Olympic dataset would raise some of the same concerns as a celebrity dataset. Parliamentarians, on the other hand, tended to be middle-aged and of various body types as representatives of the people. Nonetheless, as a former pole vaulter, I couldn't help but be drawn back to the world of sports. Teams that were already neatly categorised by country, with headshots in typically well-lit settings, on generally well-structured websites, were rather appealing. When looking at professional sports teams and visiting the NBA and WNBA websites, I was soon reminded of copyright difficulties. "Photos cannot be used without the express written consent..." The consent notice reminded me of the creepy MITRE dataset containing photographs of prisoners who had died in prison. Athletes who signed contracts with professional sports teams granted such teams permission to utilise and profit from their photographs. Those who died while confined could not have given their permission for their photographs to be used in this manner. I doubt their relatives were aware that their photographs were being used in this manner. Many of the persons included in the databases, including celebrities, were unaware of their presence. IBM was chastised for using a fraction of YFCC100M, a Yahoo dataset including 100 million pictures under a Creative Commons licence on their Flickr site. Many people were unaware that their photographs were being used in a research database that had been reused for IBM's Diversity in Faces (DiF) dataset, which used a subset of about 1 million images from YFCC100M. A person may upload an image for one purpose, such as a Flickr photo album, and their face may end up in a dataset for another. Although IBM was not alone, their dataset provided a vivid illustration of extremely typical behaviours in the sector. I began by researching the copyright policies of the parliaments I had picked. Some websites, including Rwanda's and Senegal's, had a provision that said that as public property, the website's information might be utilised for research and education purposes. I sought assistance from the Boston University Technology Law Clinic. They examined the copyright rules of all the nations I intended to target and determined that as long as I did not redistribute the dataset for profit and only used it for research purposes, I would be in the clear and inside the realm of fair use. Nonetheless, lawful use could not overcome the fact that I would be utilising photos of people's faces without their consent to conduct my research, unless I could gain the approval of the 1,270 persons who would be included in the dataset. Despite my difficulties with this question, several computer vision researchers I spoke with thought it was immaterial. Their stance was: The images are public, and they are of public officials. What exactly is your problem? I went ahead with some trepidation. The legal but heinous norm permits unethical practices. Perhaps a higher criteria was required than "What are my chances of getting sued?"

Another enigma for me was how photos of people's faces were handled. Human subjects research training was required of me in graduate school. In general, this type of study involves direct interaction with persons who will be completing surveys or interviews. The majority of the training focused on consent, privacy, and seeking to benefit the participants. The training focused on significant failures, such as the Tuskegee Syphilis Study and Nazi experimentation. The computer science researchers I met with were perplexed as to why I would require human subjects' permission for my research on how AI systems analyse human looks. Though medical photos and biometric information were classed as the type of data required for human subjects research, nonmedical photographs of faces were not. Despite the fact that universities have processes in place for research on human subjects, I was excused from undertaking computer vision research on human faces, which can serve as uniquely identifiable biometric information. I accepted the exemption and continued my research, but uncertainties remained as the deadline for my thesis approached. How can a face be deemed anonymous if it contains fundamentally unique biometric information? Was this yet another status quo that needed to be altered? Pushing for this change would make my research much more difficult, as I was unlikely to receive permission to use all of the faces I had identified for the dataset. Was I, however, any different from Facebook in my use of the faces? After all, the corporation exploited photographs supplied by individuals for facial recognition studies without gaining explicit approval. With data becoming such an important aspect of AI research and later products built on big data stores, the significance of data became increasingly clear to me. What would normally be inactive datasets could be reused in a company's endeavour to train an AI system. The data might also be sold to other companies to help them with their artificial intelligence initiatives. The Ever app, for example, began as a photo-sharing app for families. The company later evolved to provide facial recognition services, which were made feasible by photographs submitted by app users. This repurposing of data may not have been the objective of the company's founders at the outset, and users were not informed that their photographs would be utilised in this manner. Instead, like with many terms of service, users granted broad generic access to their data, enabling unknown profitable downstream use. The European Union attacked such loose data practices with the passage of the General Data Protection Regulation (GDPR), which did not extend outside Europe. None of these safeguards were fully in place when I created the dataset in 2017. Data on the internet looked to be available for free to all computer vision researchers. I had no intention of profiting from the faces I had discovered for my research. I further reasoned that because the subjects were public figures rather than private persons, they had already chosen to be in the public light. Furthermore, nothing stopped me from taking photographs and running them through AI algorithms for personal use. I downloaded photographs of parliamentarians from around the world in 2017. I requested common face datasets from other academics that had been obtained without explicit authorization through scraping websites. This was a legal procedure. Why should I feel bad? There was some substance to the notion of privacy for the photographs I ran on gender categorization and age models on my own computer, because only I had access to the data. I observed the outcomes and decided what to do with them. However, I had no idea how enterprises might exploit photos fed to distant AI systems via online demos provided by tech companies beyond the demo interfaces they provided. Using Creative Commons photographs that were uploaded to the internet did not exclude the possibility that photographers might publish images that they had taken without permission. Even if consent was provided to upload these photos, there was no affirmative approval that these images would be utilised to power data-hungry machine learning models years later.

In other words, the status quo was constructed without respect for consent. That disrespect for permission is motivated, at least in part, by expediency. If authorization is required for each image, a researcher cannot swiftly gather millions of facial images. A huge digital corporation can develop a platform for image uploading, make it part of the terms and conditions that those photographs may be utilised, and so legitimately exploit those images as desired—even without explicit authorization. I pressed on, despite these conflicts, problematic demographic and phenotypic classifications, and unconsented if nevertheless public photos of public figures. I had the categorization in hand, as well as a collection of photographs of lawmaker faces gathered from official government websites, but there was one more major step before I could utilise the data to test any AI systems. Gender and skin type labels were required for the face photos. Instead of hiring Mechanical Turk workers, I felt that 1,270 photographs was a small enough set for me to handle, despite the fact that the labour would be boring. It added to the weekend's hard fun. So many improvements in machine learning are dependent on labelled datasets, despite the headlines and glossy marketing websites. Mary L. Gray and Siddharth Suri discuss these frequently neglected labourers in their book Ghost Work, whose labour is a critical component of the machine learning process and who also support research initiatives. My classification procedure for my new dataset, which I named the Pilot Parliaments Benchmark, offered me a small taste of that job. And, while I had intended to skip the tedium and delegate data operations to an undergraduate to undertake the necessary but underappreciated and underpaid task, the process of labelling the dataset by hand gave its own insights. When I was looking through labels for my research, I discovered that the individual who decides on classification systems wields authority. After gathering a dataset in need of labelling, I was in a position to use another type of power—the power to label. It was disconcerting to classify other people's faces. My actions would have an impact on the ability to rigorously evaluate the intended gender classification systems. If my dataset selection and labels were excessively skewed (as in the previous datasets) or badly labelled, my experimental setup might be insufficient to detect any indicators of bias, even if they were present. If my dataset was not carefully designed, I would be in danger of missing the mark, much like a doctor using the wrong diagnostic equipment and so missing indicators of an illness. Nonetheless, I, like the doctor, would have the power to state, "Look, I ran a test and found no problem." I was currently serving as a second opinion on what was becoming more widely accepted in the computer vision research field on the performance of facial recognition technology. My tactics had to provide a fresh perspective in order to provide that second look. When assessing the performance of AI systems, we must consider the sorts of tests performed to reach the result, the data collection methods, the labels utilised, and who was engaged in decision-making. However, as I went over each face in my Pilot Parliaments Benchmark to establish gender and skin type, the exercise's subjectivity became clear. As more AI systems are integrated into our lives, we cannot disregard this subjectivity, and we must advocate for high standards for AI deployers to back up the claims they make about what their systems can do. We also require redlines and guardrails to prevent undesirable or unforeseen repercussions from data use. With the emergence of generative AI systems that generate images based on language prompts or supplied sample images, more mainstream discussions regarding privacy and data permission are taking place. For example, the 2022 release of the popular Lensa application's Magic Avatars feature enhanced public interest in AI-generated photos. Users may upload many photographs of their faces to the site for a price of four dollars or more, and the Magic Avatars system would return fifty or more AI-generated profile images. Celebrity, influencer, and regular people's social media accounts began to flood with stylized profile photographs that appeared to be crafted by skilled digital artists. Someone would occasionally generate images of another person. Katie Couric's husband, John Molner, for example, uploaded images of her to the app and then shared the results, which she subsequently published on social media. To bystanders and participants, the movement may have appeared to be harmless fun. What's the risk in getting styled profile photographs for less than the cost of a cup of coffee?

Shortly as the popularity of Magic Avatars grew, some women began to notice that the avatars generated for them included hypersexualized pictures. Some women received avatars depicting their likeness on barely dressed bodies or entirely topless bodies. "My avatars were cartoonishly pornified," Melissa Heikkilä wrote for the MIT Technology Review, "while my male colleagues got to be astronauts, explorers, and inventors." I doubt she and the other women expected the AI system to use information obtained from their faces to build renderings of exposed breasts when they supplied their photographs. Misogyny and the male gaze can now be utilised to deprive women of dignity in new ways thanks to AI-generated images. Campaigns against digital forms of gender-based violence, such as revenge porn, are becoming more prevalent. Revenge porn is the use of intimate photos taken with a partner, which are later circulated to humiliate or intimidate someone who meant for the images to remain private. Someone, such as a jaded lover or stalker, can use generative AI systems to generate sexualized images of you without your knowledge or agreement. Deepfakes, or AI-generated lifelike photos and videos, have previously been used to superimpose celebrities' faces onto the bodies of people conducting sexual acts without their knowledge. Users who expressed themselves about Magic Avatars, with their more cartoon-like portrayals, were not utilising the technology to create sexualized content. For example, Olivia Snow allegedly uploaded childhood photos and received sexualized representations of herself as a youngster. While this was most likely not the intention of Prisma Labs, the creators of the Lens app underlying the Magic Avatars feature, it does raise severe legal concerns in addition to ethical concerns.

Storing and disseminating child pornographic photographs and videos is a crime in the United States. Who is to blame if an AI system generates sexualized images of adults when they input childhood photos? What prevents a malicious actor from purposefully uploading a child's image in order to obtain sexualized images? At the time of writing, there are no regulations prohibiting AI systems from creating sexualized images of children. Governments and corporations alike must do more. Other AI picture producers, such as the Midjourney platform, contain capabilities such as an NSFW (not safe for work) filter, as in the case of DALL-E, a text-to-image-generation system, or community standards to avoid creating objectionable images. However, technical solutions such as the NSFW filter are not perfect, and community norms rely on participants' goodwill. Both solutions are insufficient on their own since, in the end, accountability for the development and dissemination of illegal or damaging imagery is required. Companies would be discouraged from releasing apps and features that have not been thoroughly tested and fine-tuned to prevent harmful depictions if they were punished or had their systems shut down if they produced illegal photos.

You're probably wondering how these AI graphics are created in the first place. The solution is found in datasets. Generative AI systems are trained using picture datasets acquired from the internet. LAION-5B is an open-source digital art dataset of 5.85 billion photos that comprises artwork uploaded by artists. A part of this freely available dataset was used for the Magic Avatars feature. Unknowingly, artists who contributed their work in order to advance their careers had their photos captured and used in systems such as Magic Avatars. Images posted on the internet for one purpose are frequently repurposed without explicit permission. Artists who already struggle to make a living from their artistic profession have expressed concern about their work being used to power generative AI systems. Economic concerns about the devaluation of human digital artwork, as well as legal concerns about ownership and copyrights, have given rise to websites such as Have I Been Trained (haveibeentrained.com/). This "opt-out" website allows artists to see if their work has been included in open-source datasets and to request that the data be removed. Similarly, Adam Harvey and Jules LaPlace established Exposing.ai to allow people to see if their faces were included in open-source face databases, facilitating deletion requests.

This opt-out strategy is a stopgap measure in the absence of legislation and a shift in the development of AI systems. Rather than putting the burden on users to determine whether their photographs were used in systems built without their knowledge, opting in should be the default. The corporation has already educated the AI system by the time someone discovers their photographs have been utilised, therefore deleting the image does not remove its contribution to training the AI system to accomplish a certain task. Even if the image is destroyed, the images are still present in the many copies of the dataset that have already been produced. This is why, when Meta (then Facebook) announced the removal of roughly 1 billion faceprints, there was outrage as well as joy. The jubilation centred on the fact that a major tech corporation erasing the faceprints was an acknowledgement of the risks connected with face-based technologies, which many organisations, including the AJL, had been emphasising. But we don't know if anyone within the organisation prepared a hidden backup copy, and we might never find out. Facebook's actions supplied a counternarrative to the widely held belief that once a firm obtains your data, there is nothing you can do about it. Legislation and lawsuits, as well as public pressure, make an impact.

The corporation destroyed the faceprints but not the facial recognition models that were developed with those faceprints. The corporation needed to get rid of the faceprints for legal reasons. In 2021, Facebook agreed to pay $650 million to settle charges of breaking BIPA, Illinois' Biometric Information Privacy Act. Faceprints, crucially, are produced from photos of a person's face, but they are not copies of the uploaded images. Consider your faceprint to be a digital depiction of your face. Multiple submitted pictures can be combined to create a single faceprint. As a result, a firm can remove the photographs you supplied while retaining data about your face in the form of a faceprint. That face data can be used to train AI systems by the corporation. Once the system has been educated, they can sell it or utilise it for research and development. They can then remove the facial data while keeping the AI system that has been trained.

Legislation and policies addressing user consent and data privacy must consider downstream applications. We must consider not only deleting submitted photographs and data derived from those images, such as a faceprint, but also deleting models developed with ill-gotten or repurposed data. We require deep data deletion, which entails completely erasing data obtained from user uploads as well as the AI models built on this data. Only explicitly approved data sources should be used to build commercial AI solutions. To prevent the growth of AI damages caused by the acquisition of unconsented data, we should demand deep data removals. Clearview AI, which scraped billions of images of people's faces published to public social media platforms, was fined 20 million euros by the Italian Supervisory Authority and ordered to remove the biometrics data of "persons on Italian territory." The Italian face purge is a good place to start. Deep deletions are achievable, but they will necessitate a shift in the creation, auditing, and governance of AI systems.

Downstream data usage should require explicit and affirmative consent, especially when corporations like Prisma Labs profit from the repurposed labour of nameless artists. At the time of writing, the Lens app's terms of service specify that the corporation owns the face data of users who pay for stylized photographs. According to the corporation, data is only utilised to train their internal AI system. However, nothing prevents the company from being acquired and the data from being used in unexpected ways. Another factor to consider is that many internet systems are linked to digital behemoths such as Google and Amazon. Face data is processed in part by Amazon Web Services (AWS) for the Lensa app. AWS powers a major portion of the internet and is a crucial component of internet infrastructure. AWS is used by companies such as Netflix and Zoom. As a result, you must consider not only what a single firm, such as Prisma Labs, can do with your data, but also what interconnected companies that control the computing systems that process your data can do. A network of enterprises is active in internet and app-based AI services.

Consider AI systems as an interconnected ecosystem of datasets, dispersed data processing systems provided by large tech businesses, and unsuspecting data creators that fuel the system: us. The ecosystem would collapse if we did not upload. This is not to say that it is up to individuals to tackle these problems on their own. I consider large technology corporations to be infrastructure providers, as they now offer the highways of internet networks. Because so much of modern life is centred on interacting via the internet, and governments are progressively encouraging the use of digital systems, refusing to utilise the internet is akin to wanting to live off-grid. You will almost certainly feel compelled to assist at some point, especially in emergency situations. There will be breakdowns and maintenance necessary in every large-scale infrastructure system. Some bridges created with outdated paradigms that no longer serve the modern age must be completely demolished. Others, depending on the circumstances, may be reconstructed. We do not urge people to stop using roads when they point out potholes that could cause dangerous accidents or illustrate the damage done to their vehicles as a result of a pothole. We also do not expect individuals to repair potholes on their own. Instead, we seek out organisations that have been formed to protect the public interest and maintain infrastructure. The duty for averting AI damages does not lay with individual users, but with the firms that develop these systems, the organisations that adopt them, and the elected officials charged with protecting the public interest. Individually, we may tell our stories, document injuries, and insist that our dignity be a priority, not an afterthought. We may exercise caution before partaking in AI trends such as styled profile photographs, and we can support organisations that put pressure on firms and policymakers to prevent AI damages.

CHAPTER 9
GENDER SHADES

While no one has a monopoly on truth, some corporations in the technology sector control a sizable chunk of the ecosystem. These digital titans have huge resources and have a significant impact on our daily lives. Google's search engine serves as a portal to the world's internet knowledge, collecting vital search history data while serving up revenue advertisements. Microsoft's Windows operating system is a mainstay in many organisations that use the software that comes standard with the majority of personal PCs. IBM, the big blue company, pioneered enterprise and government IT solutions. Amazon is a technology behemoth that has figured out how to dominate several areas of e-commerce while also providing technological solutions to other businesses via Amazon Web Services. I had to tread carefully in the domain of these giants. These corporations frequently provided funding for AI research at prestigious institutions. It didn't escape my notice that the Stata Center at MIT, which housed the Computer Science Artificial Intelligence Lab, had a Gates wing named after Microsoft's founder. Some firms, such as Google, IBM, and Microsoft, offered fellowships that paid for or greatly reduced the cost of completing graduate studies in computer science. Top students who completed a computer science degree found competitive and appealing job offers from IT behemoths, who were assured of a consistent supply of bright research talent. The shadow of the tech titans permeated many facets of the AI research ecosystem, from funding specific areas of research to providing the resources to pursue pricey graduate degrees and offering attractive tech sector jobs. Getting on the wrong side of one of these companies could have major ramifications for your career. However, as a PhD student, I had little interest in working for one of them. My tuition was totally paid for, and I received a stipend. The Media Lab's financing structure, particularly my association with the Center for Civic Media, afforded me greater leeway than most graduate students exploring AI systems. Ethan, my advisor, was also not obligated to any of these tech businesses to actively fund our research. Ethan instead sought funding from foundations such as the Ford Foundation, the Knight Foundation, and the Robert Wood

Johnson Foundation. All of this to say, when it came time to choose target systems to evaluate for algorithmic bias, I didn't feel constrained in my choices. I was curious to see if a more varied dataset may reveal flaws that others had overlooked. It was time to choose my targets now that I had my designated Pilot Parliaments Benchmark in hand. For the commercial systems, I concentrated on businesses who have public demonstrations with explicit gender classification available on their websites. Because of this focus, IBM, Microsoft, and Face++ were chosen. At the time, you could upload photographs to IBM's Watson project via the IBM website, and you could upload images to Microsoft's Azure demo website via the Microsoft website. Because of China's significant role in AI development, I included the Face++ system from the Chinese company Megvii. Prior research had shown that systems designed in China performed differently on Western and Asian faces, so I wanted to investigate whether there were any discrepancies in test results from companies located in the United States and ones based in China. According to marketing materials, the company had an online demo that was free to the public and was also used by numerous developers. While these companies all provided public demos, which I used to gauge their confidence in their product, manually uploading 1,270 photographs would be impractical. To perform the study, I created accounts so that I could access their systems using code I wrote. The code sent each image from the Pilot Parliaments Benchmark to IBM, Microsoft, and Face++ for processing remotely. Once each photograph was processed, I would receive the findings, which would provide some indication of the detected face as well as educated predictions about age, gender, and other attributes based on what the particular business supplied. I choose to focus simply on gender in order to keep the study as simple as possible. The Pilot Parliaments Benchmark that I developed at MIT was tiny but powerful enough to reveal substantial flaws and gaps in the evaluation of machine learning models. Other notable benchmarks often had tens of thousands of photographs on the low end and millions of images on the high end. You don't have to do anything just because you can. Less is more in some cases. With the IBM classifier, the intersectional analysis revealed that the highest discrepancy in accuracy was up to 34.4 percent between lighter males and darker females. Such a discrepancy in performance was not reflected in IBM's overall performance of 87.9 percent accuracy on the benchmark. This type of disparity would not be visible in IBM's 14.7 percent gender gap or 9.2 percent skin type gap. The various patterns highlight the significance of investigating specific systems because we cannot predict which way intersectional analysis will fall. What accuracy does not reveal are concerns about failure. How are errors spread when a system fails? We should not assume that errors are distributed evenly. Beyond only looking at a system's accuracy, we may learn more about performance by looking at the types of errors that are committed. For error analysis, I went a step farther and examined the findings by skin type, which revealed even lower performance. When I looked at women with the darkest skin on the Fitzpatrick skin type scale, I discovered that mistake rates for female-labelled faces of type VI may reach 46.8 percent. To my knowledge, these were among the largest accuracy discrepancies reported for commercially sold AI solutions at the time. My test had revealed severe flaws in the system not only from modest research laboratories, but also from some of the most venerable and well-known technology companies. What other biases could be hiding in the tech giants' AI products if they had bias in gender classification?

I was finally making my way to the Hayden Library after two years on the MIT campus. I had yet to visit a college library, despite having internet access to practically all of the materials I required. I felt ready to submit my master's thesis after printing results on archival paper that felt soft yet durable to the touch and hunting down last-minute mistakes. Throughout the summer of 2017, I flipped back and forth between datasets, spreadsheets, and calculations. I eagerly emailed my findings to my committee members, who astonished me with their comments in the margins. I paid Hal Abelson a visit. "Your calculations show accuracy differences, but what's the harm?" "Why should people be concerned?" Hal's inquiries lingered with me. "Is being misclassified harmful?" "Does it matter if a parliament member is misgendered?" Perhaps the example I chose was not convincing enough, or perhaps having an all-male committee made them less sensitive to the consequences of misgendering women?

This felt to me like saying, "She was hit by a brick; look at the evidence," and then being asked, "How do we know being hit by a brick is harmful?"

I couldn't expect that everyone would recognize that the issue with gender classification was significant in and of itself, as well as a sign that similar concerns could arise in other areas of facial recognition technologies and AI. Being unfairly arrested and misclassified as a criminal suspect sounded high stakes to me. The deep learning techniques used to generate gender classifiers were also employed to create systems that attempted to identify a unique individual or detect skin cancer. All of these systems had to be evaluated for algorithmic bias. There were also costs to dignity as a result of gender misclassification, but such harms did not appear to affect the members of my committee. I was dissatisfied since outcomes that I thought were significant now appeared to be lessened. Maybe I was exaggerating what I had discovered. Perhaps this was part of an academic rite of passage in which you had to defend the significance of your work to a sceptical audience of older academics.

I posed my own questions to Hal and the rest of the committee. "Should I show the faces of those who are mislabeled?" The committee didn't see anything wrong with it, but exposing the mislabeled faces immediately didn't sit well with me. It seemed like I was going to frame an insult directed at someone. When I gave particular data on errors, I opted to show average faces, composite photographs that blended numerous people together so that no specific identification could be seen. "Should the thesis's focus be on algorithmic bias or dataset bias?" I also questioned my committee. In other words, was the study more about data or the algorithms used to create the gender classifiers I tested? The answer evolved over time to be both. The skews in benchmark datasets created a false impression of progress, and existing popular datasets had biases that needed to be properly named. Yes, the dataset affects the gender categorization systems based on machine learning models, but preprocessing stages like face detection could bring bias into the process as well. Subsequent study revealed that for some systems, even when datasets were more equal in the training phase, results were skewed, indicating that data was not the sole piece of the jigsaw. Hal taught me during the summer that I couldn't presume that everyone would regard gender classification or misclassification as detrimental. He was pressuring me to provide additional context and explain why the work was important. He also prepared me for the scepticism expressed by others in the computer science community. At the same time, I wasn't only working for the computer science community; I was also working for individuals who would find themselves on the wrong side of a label. Hal advised me to underline that the techniques employed for gender classification were also applied in other fields of computer vision and machine learning, and that these findings should be interpreted as a red flag. "This might seem obvious to you, but you are going to need to draw the connections so people understand what you are talking about." Though the findings focused on gender classifications, the ramifications have broader significance. Nonetheless, I did not wish to downplay the significance of misclassification. I remembered all the humiliating moments as a child when I was asked if I was a male or a girl, or when I was supposed to be a boy. I also didn't want misclassification to be interpreted as a demand to just improve gender classifiers, but rather to examine the enterprise of identifying people in the first place. These considerations would be discussed on an ongoing basis. For the time being, I had a master's thesis to do. I saw Dr. Ruchir Puri, the chief scientist at IBM Research, on my way to Hayden Library on the MIT campus. We had met earlier in the summer at the second Aspen Institute Roundtable on Artificial Intelligence, where I had briefly shared my research topic with him and enjoyed our talk about the future of AI. I started walking quickly across the red bricks that accentuated the familiar pathways. "Ruchir! Ruchir!" I yelled, holding up my bound papers. My thesis is being submitted. "You'll want to see the IBM results." He came to a halt and turned around with his two girls. With fatherly pride, he introduced them to me, and then said with expectation. "Send me a copy!"

I'd finally send the results to Ruchir. I had decided to continue my academic career by the time I completed my master's thesis and had been accepted into the MIT Media Lab PhD program with Ethan as my advisor. However, Ethan was taking a year off to work on a new book, so I would be spending the entire year with Mitch Resnick's Lifelong Kindergarten group. With my master's thesis completed, I could devote the first semester of my PhD program to publishing the "Gender Shades" findings.

The timing couldn't have been more perfect. The Conference on Fairness, Accountability, and Transparency in AI had been announced that summer. They were asking for proposals for the inaugural conference, which would be held in February 2018. Timnit and I cooperated to submit the "Gender Shades" paper to the conference. While some reviewers questioned the uniqueness of the findings and the need to employ the Fitzpatrick classification systems, the research was eventually accepted. A peer-reviewed publication was a huge success for me as a graduate student. It lent more credibility to my thesis work. I also believed it would make the tech businesses take me seriously when I sought out them. Now with an accepted paper, I began discussing the results with all the companies. I emailed IBM's Ruchir as well as Microsoft and Face++ personnel, since their companies were all implicated by the report. I heard back from Ruchir pretty immediately. He wanted to know who the competition was. I had delivered the paper results with all the findings, but instead of mentioning the firm names I used companies A, B, and C. They would have to wait until the conference to know for sure who their competitors were. In the meantime, IBM took a fairly assertive attitude. Since I was not distributing the Pilot Parliaments Benchmark dataset, they created an internal dataset of their own and shared with me that they had observed similar findings. They invited me to their New York office on January 26, 2018, to speak to a number of executives. A few days after turning twenty-eight, I walked toward the IBM Watson building in New York City. I was greeted by a large metallic red balloon dog. The Jeff Koons statue welcomed me to corporate America. After passing the security guards and rows of cubicles, I entered a clearing that looked like a small amphitheatre, where I would walk through my research findings. I presented the "Gender Shades" work to Ruchir Puri, IBM chief scientist; Francesca Rossi, head of AI and Ethics; Anna Sekaran, head of communications; and members of the computer vision team, who sat nervously as I advanced through the slides showing performance results.

"Who are the other companies?" they queried.

"You are going to have to wait and see…"

After the formal presentation, I enjoyed lunch with the team. Again I was asked, "Who are the other companies?"

The food was adequate but not exceptional. "You will have to wait and see."

Later that evening, I went out to eat with a couple IBMers who had been on the drill team analysing my study for a genuinely fantastic Italian meal. "Who are the other companies?" I was asked for the third time. I almost slipped when I took another spoonful of noodles, but I stopped myself.

"You are going to have to wait and see…"

I enjoyed teasing the IBMers about the unnamed competition and talking shop with the computer vision team. Obviously, I wasn't there to try to land a job at IBM after graduation. One of the participants offered a tip: "You know, when we replicated your approach and ran it on our old model, our results were even worse than what you reported." I forced a smile. I purposefully constructed the study so that when others duplicated it, the outcomes would most likely be worse. In the scholarly study, I did not publish the worst-case scenario findings. Following the NYC meeting, I had many meetings at the IBM Boston headquarters. The team informed me that they had created a new model and wanted me to present the findings at the conference. I insisted on testing their new model at my workplace, so they drove to the Media Lab and met me immediately around the corner from the Foodcam. As they strolled past the ping-pong table in the atrium, their attire gave off a corporate vibe. The IBM team members shared their model with me while sitting next to my LEGOs, surrounded by grad school memorabilia and the white mask. The results were noticeably better than the previous model. One of the computer vision team members clasped his hands in prayer and looked me in the eyes. "Please share the updated results." I recognized the gleam in his eyes. His reputation was at stake. Just as there are people whose lives are influenced by the labels and classifications generated by machine learning systems, there are people whose professions and livelihoods are related to the items I was investigating. Prior to my travels to the

IBM premises, the developers of these commercial systems were as faceless to me as the consumers impacted by these systems were to them. In some ways, they were "just" doing their jobs as they had been instructed to do. But when simply doing your job can mean putting someone else's life in danger, there has to be a higher standard. Performing your duties does not excuse harm. He was looking at me with pleading eyes, saying, "We can do better." He reminded me of one of my father's postdocs, who came to our house and helped set up the Silicon Graphics machines that had intrigued me as a child. The majority of my father's students, like us, were immigrants. As the daughter of an immigrant scholar, I wondered what my father would be like in that situation. What if my father worked for a corporation? What if his livelihood and capacity to maintain our family were jeopardised, as well as his reputation in a field he had committed decades to? Would I be willing to reveal his most recent results? My engineering side could relate with the difficulties of developing functional systems. I just had a few weeks to process these ideas and make a decision.

CHAPTER 10
DESERTED DESSERTS

I relaxed into my chair as I put my book bag beneath the seat in front of me, preparing to travel from Boston to New York City for the second time in two months. I was on my way to give "Gender Shades'' its first public academic paper presentation at the first FacT Conference, a computer science conference that brings together researchers and engineers interested in fairness, accountability, and transparency in technology. My excitement was growing within me. I adjusted my slides several times and practised what I would say out loud, hoping not to disturb the person sitting next to me. I was making my way through the academic hoops necessary to one day become Dr. Buolamwini: Check. Master's thesis. Acceptance into a PhD program—check. Check for a published academic study. The presentation of the conference paper is still awaited. New York University hosted the conference. I entered the reception area after obtaining a registration badge at the front desk. A few tables were piled high with bran muffins, grapes, cheese cubes, and other typical conference fare. I began to recognize scholars whose work I had read about after selecting some food to snack on. My chats with Cathy O'Neil and Timnit assured me that I was not alone, and I wanted to meet additional supporters in this emerging field of study at this conference. The reception hall was packed with researchers, sponsors, and the occasional press, indicating the growing interest in algorithmic bias research. Dr. Latanya Sweeney delivered the keynote address. Her work created the intellectual groundwork for mine. In 2013, she released "Discrimination in Online Ad Delivery," a widely influential research that proved racial prejudice in search engine rankings. The study found that search results for names more likely to be given to Black kids had a higher chance of displaying an arrest record advertisement than names more likely to be given to White babies. The ad implied that the person with the name had been captured by police, but this did not have to be the case. The ramifications of this alarming tendency are easy to imagine: If a landlord or hiring manager searched for an applicant's name and then discovered a link to an arrest record advertisement, they may decide to pass on the candidate consciously or unintentionally. Given racial perceptions about Black Americans and criminality, such advertisements could contribute to confirmation bias. The article identified both allocative effects and representational harms linked with stigma. Allocative harms are the deprivation of tangible goods or opportunities, such as employment or housing. Representational harms are associated with the stories and pictures that circulate about who and what is wrong in society. Sweeney gently informed the audience during her conference remarks that day that they should learn more about the work of a fresh up-and-coming researcher. She then motioned to me, and I smiled uncomfortably as heads turned to look at me. Her encouragement was appreciated, but I also felt more pressure to live up to her praise. Timnit and I enjoyed dinner at a local cafe the night before my presentation.

"Should we present this together?" I inquired of her.

"No, you're the primary author. The paper is also based on your master's thesis. I'll be cheering you on from the stands. "Aside from that, are you going to that dinner?"

I'd received an email inviting me to dinner with one of the conference sponsors, but I was still undecided. Cathy O'Neil was in New York, and her bluegrass band was performing. Perhaps I could do both. I was sleeping in a tight Airbnb with another Media Lab student, seeking for any excuse to spend as little time as possible in the little flat.

"I'm considering it." "Are you planning on going?"

"Only if you come with me."

I draw out my black-and-white ajl shield the next morning. I wore my reflective translucent yellow eyeglass spectacles and yellow feather earrings to commemorate the event. I appeared to be a canary in a sea of black, navy, and grey-clad professors, rather than a computer vision researcher. My chest clenched as I approached the podium. I pushed through the emotion and began the presentation, telling the narrative of the white mask demo. I discussed the shortcomings of current gold standards and how power shadows haunt the field. Then I moved on to the research findings, starting with general accuracy and progressing to gender accuracy, skin type accuracy, and lastly intersectional accuracy. I looked up from my laptop and searched the audience once I reached the results with the IBM slides. IBM's Francesca Rossi sat near the front row, her eyes wide with excitement.

"IBM was the most responsive of all the companies I contacted." They reproduced the study and, just a few weeks ago, released a new model."

I used the clicker to progress the slides.

"Here are their results."

"Previously, IBM performed at 65.3 percent accuracy on darker females; according to their internal tests, the new model performs at 96.5 percent." "Change is a possibility."

I concluded that because IBM made the effort to participate in the research, it was appropriate for me to publish their updated results as they had requested. Perhaps the company might use its clout to persuade other businesses to conduct internal algorithmic audits. Perhaps there was room for a public-private cooperation after all. When I finished the talk, the pressure in my chest dissipated. As my gaze met Tinnitus, I could hear the audience applaud. Her smile lit up the entire front row. That evening, fueled by the buzz surrounding the "Gender Shades' ' study, I decided to accompany Timnit to the business dinner. When we arrived, we were shown to a private room with rich, velvet-lined walls that was intended for special gatherings. We were free to choose our seats, so I sat in the centre, directly across from the host. To begin the dinner and acknowledge prominent visitors, the host cleared his throat. "Everyone gathered here is fighting to shape the future of artificial intelligence." "We have power."

When it was my turn to speak, I questioned the host, saying, "Not everyone here has the same power, certainly not the same power as you." Timnit agreed with a nod. Senior scholars requesting support from the corporate sponsor shifted their gaze uneasily around the table. The host, obviously unaffected by my statements, initiated a discussion about the future of AI. I felt disconnected from my Media Lab workplace, where I fantasised about being among the decision-makers. I had a seat at the table now, and I wasn't going to waste it. "We must harness AI for good!" exclaimed a person at the far end of the table. Consider the people of Africa.... I've been there for a while, and we need to make sure we're thinking about AI from their point of view." I was surprised to hear a familiar voice at the other end of the table. "I consider Africa. I am a refugee from Ethiopia. We have far too many so-called experts parachuting in ideas. Locals have essential knowledge and are aware of what is going on. They, not white saviours, should lead the work!" Dinner guests were enjoying much more than a delicious feast, as we moved our heads back and forth like spectators at a tennis match. Polite discourse was extinct. The person seated next to me had been nervously cutting away at a piece of steak in the middle of the back-and-forth. They finally got through the meat, only for the final cut to catapult at the host. Thud!

Our host was not amused, but he kept his cool a little longer. Meg Mitchell, a prolific AI researcher with red hair and a fiery tongue, joined the heated discussion, questioning whether the sponsor's plan to work with health data may lead to some ugly ethical implications. The host has had enough. He announced that he needed to leave after thanking everyone who had come. Other dinner guests found reasons to leave as well. I took a look at the printed menu beside my fork and copper cup. One course was not provided. Timnit, Meg, and a few constantly hungry graduate students joined me in staying. The servers entered the room, balancing dishes full of tantalising goodies. Every seat, including the recently abandoned ones, had a dessert plate meticulously set on it. We had our pick of deserted desserts once the servers left: exquisite chocolate mousse, cheesecakes, and more. I had a lot to think about. As we moved through the desserts, I thought about my own part in parachuting in ideas. AI was being introduced into the world by well-meaning firms and academics with enormous clout with the intention of doing good. "You are some of the world's smartest people, creating some of the most powerful technology known to mankind," an ecstatic dinner guest exclaimed. You should put it to good use. You should take on the most difficult challenges. This is a fantastic opportunity." The desire to employ technology for good was a well-known moral imperative. When I was nineteen years old, I devised a life mission to accomplish good in the world and achieve my own potential: to demonstrate compassion through computation. I had worked at the Carter Center as an undergraduate to study on neglected tropical diseases, specifically trachoma. Trachoma is a preventable disease that used to cause blindness in countries such as the United States. It had now been exterminated in many parts of the world, but a few tenacious enclaves remained in Ethiopia and elsewhere. The trachoma initiative appealed to me because the problem was manageable. A medicine named Zithromax was found to be effective in preventing the sickness. However, the medication had to be distributed in rural locations that were frequently difficult to reach, and finance was always an issue. The Carter Center struck an agreement with Pfizer and joined forces with Ethiopian officials to eradicate trachoma. I observed a bronze statue of a youngster leading a blind elder using the stick they both grasped as I strolled through the gardens of the Jimmy Carter Presidential Library in Atlanta, Georgia. Sightless Among Miracles was given to the centre to highlight the endeavour to aid in the global control of onchocerciasis (river blindness). There was reason to be optimistic: The Carter Center team was on its way to eradicating river blindness in a number of nations through collaborative efforts. Trachoma was next on the Carter Center's short-term agenda. The centre had systems in place to monitor and assess their activities in order to track the effectiveness of the campaign. This is when I come into the story—my first attempt at "saving the world." Their evaluations were conducted on paper surveys, which were later digitised through transcription. If you looked at my day-to-day activities, you might conclude that I was simply creating digital surveys. To me, I was fighting for the world and assisting in the eradication of neglected tropical illnesses through the use of revolutionary mobile data collection methodologies. At least, this is what I would state in a subsequent Rhodes Scholarship application. You are making a significant contribution to an important global health endeavour. This is what I told myself when the work became monotonous. During the summer of my junior year, I travelled to Ethiopia to test the MALTRA (malaria and trachoma) mobile surveying application. I created the application to help improve the error-prone procedure of gathering paper-based surveys. We arrived in Kombolcha, a town in Ethiopia's Amhara region, after many flights and long hours in a Carter Center four-wheel drive passing shepherds, some with guns and others with staffs, and groups wrapped in white textiles that framed their gorgeous faces. It was time to put the system through its paces. While our hosts informed us that there would be internet access, the connection speed was slower than expected. In the evening, while coding under a mosquito net, I changed the system to save data locally. As I had hoped, I would not be able to submit the data straight to an internet database. I'd developed the system in my playroom in my suburban childhood home in Cordova, Tennessee, earlier that summer. However, the assumptions I made in Cordova did not hold up in Kombolcha. At the time, the Google Android tablets I was developing did not have Amharic keyboards, despite the fact that the majority of the individuals being surveyed and the health personnel required Amharic. For the Android tablets that had to be put onto each new device, our project team created a bespoke Amharic keyboard. Defaults are not impartial. Years later, I ran into some Android project members and inquired as to why Amharic keyboards were not accessible at the time. The solution was business economics. Ethiopia was not a priority market for Google. Who will decide our priorities in the age of AI? What assumptions about utilising AI for good are being made by people who are far away from the realities of those they hope to assist? My desire to offer compassion through computing had to be balanced against my lack of knowledge about what would genuinely assist. I'd taken a parachute approach, jumping into an unknown spot. Though I like to think that I made a significant contribution to the Carter Center's data collection efforts, my experience in Ethiopia demonstrated the limits of good intentions and the need for local context. The Ethiopia experience had taught me that technology alone was insufficient. Instead of debating whether we should use a resistive or capacitive touch screen mobile tablet, I began to wonder why I had travelled to Ethiopia to work on this project rather than having locals undertake the technical development work. A few years later, as part of my continued mission to convey compassion through computation, I completed a Fulbright scholarship focused on empowering Zambian youth to create meaningful mobile applications. Sub-Saharan Fulbrighters gathered in Addis Ababa in 2013, exchanging experiences and hearing program administrators warn us that when we came home, we would be regarded as experts on our host countries. One of our Ethiopian hosts, on the other hand, reminded us that after just seven or so months in a country, we couldn't legitimately claim to be experts and that we needed to come in with the mindset of asking what the people who live here are already doing. Deficits in my thinking were gradually revealed.

Later on, I became acquainted with the effective altruism movement, which was gaining traction about the time I began my Rhodes Scholarship at the University of Oxford. Proponents of effective altruism urged soon-to-be grads to do their homework and donate to organisations that will have the most impact, rather than merely those that will make them feel good. One method could be the "earn to give" route, which involves seeking a prosperous profession in investment banking in order to have more money to donate to organisations deemed effective by trusted partners. The framing seemed first appealing. What's wrong with conducting research to optimise the influence of a person's discretionary income for those who are fortunate enough to do so? Cause triage, or absolute priority, demanded a utilitarian approach of achieving the most benefit for the greatest number of people while ignoring the issue of injustice. Good is likewise ill-defined, ambiguous enough to imply positive purpose but defined in a quantitative fashion that prioritises scale over intimacy, with little respect for what cannot be quantified or counted.

My issue with effective altruism is that it entrenches the existing quo. Supporting exclusive charities avoids addressing the issues that lead to the formation of charities in the first place and does not necessitate changing current power dynamics or business practices. The movement developed beyond advocating for bed nets, such as those given as part of the MALTRA program, to considering hazards and effects to future humanity. The logic went something like this: In the future, trillions of humans are possible, and we have an obligation to protect those beings as best we can.

This worldview, known as "long termism," with adherents known as longtermists, holds that we have an obligation to be decent ancestors, to consider what we owe the future and act accordingly. This point of view is directly at odds with the growth of artificial intelligence. Sure, there could be short-term consequences from algorithmic bias, such as what was discovered in the "Gender Shades" article, but an even bigger issue for long-termism is thinking about the existential threats AI poses to hypothetical humans who do not yet exist. In other words, long-termists are concerned about the possibility that AI systems would outsmart the humans in control of economic and political systems, causing harm to billions of people. According to the logic, the rise of the robots could be the fall of man, and thus constitutes an existential threat that we must prepare for now. I'm curious if the worry is that more people will be injured, or if those in power now fear being sidelined by modern technology. This rise of machine overlords would replace the current human overlords, whose decisions already have a negative influence on billions of people. Longtermists follow in the tradition of caring for future generations. Many ancient cultures highlighted the significance of caring for the world so that future generations can breathe clean air and drink from nature's bounty. However, protecting future generations entails addressing current and manageable threats.

Longtermist thinking isn't limited to eccentrics' late-night musings. For example, Oxford philosopher Nick Bostrom proposed the paper clip thought experiment to demonstrate why he thinks in the necessity to create strategies to protect against machine-generated superintelligence. The thought experiment goes as follows: When humans assign a goal to an AI system, we do not have complete control over how that AI system achieves that goal. Bostrom contends that if the goal is to generate as many paper clips as possible, the AI's path to do so is dangerous. A sufficiently evolved AI agent may use its intelligence to persuade powerful persons to divert resources and influence priorities in order to maximise paper clip manufacturing. Paper clip manufacturing, like computer vision systems mistaking blueberry muffins for chihuahuas, may appear insignificant, trivial, or cute at best. These ideas and examples, however, are presented in elite institutions, used in college curricula, and shared in a way that impacts the discourse about the future of AI by individuals being groomed to hold influential positions in companies, governments, and academia. Concerns about the potential hazards of artificial intelligence (AI) based on the rise of AGI with intellect superior to humans have given rise to a field known as AI safety. Anthropic, a 2021 AI safety business, acquired more than $700 million in funding in less than eighteen months. What if equivalent resources were committed to real AI harms that are neither hypothetical nor distant?

The phrase "x-risk" refers to the imagined existential peril presented by AI. While my research supports why AI systems should not be linked into weapons systems due to the fatal threats, this is not because I believe AI systems as superintelligent beings constitute an existential risk. AI systems incorrectly identifying humans as criminal suspects, policing robots, and self-driving cars with defective pedestrian tracking systems can already endanger your life. Unfortunately, we do not need AI systems to be superintelligent for them to be lethal to individual lives. Because they are real, existing AI systems with demonstrable damages are more hazardous than speculative "sentient" AI systems. One disadvantage of underestimating real AI problems by claiming that potential existential harms are more relevant is that it changes the flow of precious resources and legislative attention. Companies who profess to be concerned about the existential threat posed by AI may demonstrate a genuine commitment to saving mankind by refusing to release the AI technologies they allege would end humanity. I'm not opposed to blocking the development of lethal AI systems. Governments worried about the harmful use of AI systems can implement the restrictions long advocated for by the Campaign to Stop Killer Robots, such as the prohibition of lethal autonomous systems and digital dehumanisation. The advertising discusses potentially lethal applications of AI without making the exaggerated claim that we are on the verge of creating sentient computers capable of annihilating humanity.

Though it is tempting to see physical violence as the ultimate evil, doing so allows us to overlook the destructive ways in which our communities sustain structural violence. This concept was coined by Johan Galtung to describe how institutions and social systems prohibit people from achieving their basic wants and hence cause suffering. Individual harms and generational scars are perpetuated when individuals are denied access to healthcare, housing, and work due to the usage of AI. AI systems have the potential to slowly murder mankind.

Given what the "Gender Shades" findings revealed about algorithmic bias from some of the world's leading tech companies, my concern was about the immediate problems and emerging vulnerabilities with AI that we could address in ways that would also contribute to a future in which the burdens of AI did not fall disproportionately on the marginalised and vulnerable. AI systems with poor intelligence that result in wrongful arrests or incorrect diagnoses must be rectified immediately. Similarly, the passionate dinner guest was concerned with addressing near-term AI challenges. They left dinner early because they needed to advise on a biometric identity scheme in another country. What if the desire to do good with AI leads to the deployment of parachutes with holes on thankless and unwanted missions?

Looking across the table and thinking about how many people would never be invited to a dinner like this, I wondered if I would be invited to any more private dinners. I considered the excoded—people who are currently being damaged and those who are at risk of being harmed by AI systems.

When I consider x-risk, I also consider the risk and reality of being excluded. When a hospital employs AI for triage and leaves you without care, or when a clinical algorithm prevents you from receiving a life-saving organ transplant, you may be excluded. When you are rejected a loan due to algorithmic decision-making, you may be excluded. When your resume is automatically screened out and you are denied the ability to compete for the remaining jobs that are not replaced by AI systems, you are encoded. When a tenant screening algorithm refuses you access to housing, you may be excluded. These are all true examples. No one is immune to being excluded, and those who are already marginalised are more vulnerable.

During this dinner, I recognized that my research could not be limited to company insiders, AI researchers, or even well-intentioned influencers. Academic conferences were, indeed, major venues. For many academics, presenting published papers was the pinnacle of a particular scholarly investigation. Presenting "Gender Shades" at New York University was a springboard for me. I felt driven to put my research into action after leaving the island of delectable desserts, beyond talking shop with AI practitioners, academic lectures, and private dinners. Reaching out to academics and industry insiders was simply insufficient. I needed to make sure that ordinary people who were at risk of being harmed by AI were included in the fight for algorithmic justice.

CHAPTER 11
AI, AIN'T I A WOMAN?

I detected a gap. Research articles could reach academics and AI practitioners in the industry, but I wanted something more to reach the general public. I also needed to reach decision-makers, such as elected officials, who may be swayed by AI's promises of enhanced efficiency while being unaware of racial, gender, and other sorts of bias. Did Indian government authorities considering the Aadhaar system be aware of the possibility for bias in the biometric solutions being provided as solutions for effective allocation of government resources and persistent identification? Did they realise that algorithmic bias may deny benefits to the same people they were attempting to assist? What about police departments implementing face recognition software? What, if anything, did they know about algorithmic bias? I knew I couldn't rely on the firms marketing these products to point out their faults. There was no reason to include technology flaws in a sales pitch. I needed to personalise the dangers and prejudices of AI systems and present a viewpoint that tech corporations were likely to avoid. How can I utilise my knowledge to help others get past the headlines about my work, "Facial Recognition Is Accurate, If You're a White Guy," and experience the impact on a single person?

I believed that testing the faces of the Black Panther cast would be a good way to humanise AI biases and make the topic more mainstream than an academic article. Because my study revealed that the systems I tested performed the worst on the faces of darker-skinned females, I decided to focus on the faces of Wakanda's women: Lupita Nyong'o as Nakia, Letitia Wright as Shuri, Angela Bassett as Queen Ramonda, and Danai Gurira as courageous General Okoye. I hired Deborah Raji as my research intern to do a small-scale audit of the Black Panther cast's faces across five organisations' AI systems. The Black Panther Face Scorecard initiative grew out of this investigation. The project showed several parallels with my own life. Some of their faces, like mine, were misgendered, not identified at all, or, in some cases, mis-aged. Angela Bassett, who was in her late fifties at the time of the photograph, was estimated to be between the ages of eighteen and twenty-four by IBM's system. (Perhaps not every algorithmic bias was that bad.)

The outcomes were entertaining. The Black Panther Face Scorecard generated grins from coworkers and guests from MIT Media Lab member firms. These imaginary characters, performed by actors whose faces had been seen by billions, nonetheless felt secure from everyday reality. While more ladies were sporting shorn heads, few people were seen wearing vibranium undershirts or bracelets containing bullets to keep superhero families safe. This, at least, was not happening in my social circles. My interest was piqued by the performance numbers for Wakandan women. How will these AI systems perform on the faces of legendary women from the past and present, not simply imaginary dark-skinned women? How could AI interpret the faces of famous women like Michelle Obama, Serena Williams, and Oprah Winfrey?

And how would it fare with historical characters such as Sojourner Truth, who escaped slavery by purchasing her freedom and advocated for women's rights and the end of slavery? I was particularly excited to try on the masks of Shirley Chisholm, the first Black congressman, and Ida B. Wells, the fearless journalist. Deborah Raji ran my search for popular, extensively used photographs of these women through platforms such as IBM, Amazon, and Microsoft. I was astounded when she revealed the results. It was one thing to look at the names with the results in a spreadsheet. Seeing the faces of ladies I adored and respected next to labels with grossly inaccurate descriptions like "clean shaven adult man" was an unusual sensation. As I read the results, I kept shaking my head, mortified that my personal icons were being classed in this fashion by AI algorithms. When I saw Serena Williams being branded "male," I remembered being asked as a child, "Are you a boy or a girl?" When I saw an image of a school-aged Michelle Obama with the word "toupee," I remembered the harsh chemicals I had to apply on my head to straighten my kinky curls, and I resolved to embrace my natural hair. And seeing a photograph of a young Oprah with no face detected reminded me of my white mask experience. For a time, I tried to distance myself from my research findings, which revealed that all systems evaluated performed the worst for dark-skinned girls. Other groupings, such as darker-skinned males and lighter-skinned females, were mentioned in the study. With my most recent examination of women I liked, I had the opportunity to bring dark-skinned women like myself to the forefront. I had the ability to give faces to what would otherwise be faceless outlines. My initial thought was to make an explanatory film similar to the one I did for the "Gender Shades" study paper. That felt familiar and comfy. It enabled me to demonstrate some of the ridiculous results from the perspective of an analyst, explaining how the results mirrored misogynoir, a term coined by Dr. Moya Bailey to describe how Black women, in particular, are ridiculed or discriminated against. I gave the draft script for an explanatory video on these iconic ladies to a teaching assistant in a film class I visited on a regular basis and asked how I could improve it. "What motivated you to work on it?" he inquired.

"The research paper starts a conversation, but the results are abstract." I don't want to diminish the humanity of the experience of being misgendered, of being classified in ways over which you have no influence. I want people to understand what it means when systems from digital behemoths confine us to preconceptions that we thought to transcend using algorithms. "I want people to bear witness to the labels and peer for themselves into the coded gaze."

He bowed his head as I talked.

"Have you considered making a poem about this instead of a script?"

For years, there was a type of art that I liked but kept mostly to myself. I kept poetry and phrases in notebooks and digital diaries. Snippets of my poetry lingered in the shadows. I liked writing, but it was largely a private, vulnerable activity for me: I'd planned to keep my poems mostly to myself and a small network of sympathetic listeners.

The following sentence sat in my thoughts as the sunlight warmed me awake the next morning, encapsulating how I felt about watching the cultural effect of Serena Williams, Michelle Obama, and Oprah Winfrey travelling in their paths:

My heart smiles as I bask in their legacy, knowing that their lives changed many people's lives.

More words came to mind while I washed my teeth and peered into a fogged mirror:

I see my mother's poise in her eyes.

I see my auntie's grace in her face.

More sentences came to me as I pondered the work: Can machines ever see my queens as I see them?

Can machines ever see our grandmothers the way we remember them?

"AI, Ain't I A Woman?" became my poetry. The piece included sentiments that I had long suppressed. My grief and disappointment came to the surface as I read the poem aloud. However, for the full impact, the comments had to be combined with the photographs and depressing labels put on these iconic women by AI systems from top tech corporations. Seeing me transform myself by donning a white mask to be seen to a machine was part of what made the white mask demo more effective than words alone. I used to think of tech demonstrations as celebrations of what machines could do until I made the white mask fail demo. If a demonstration ended in failure, the demo gods would let you down. I remembered Steve Jobs, dressed in a black turtleneck, not only talking about the possibilities of an iPhone, but also demonstrating them with carefully chosen instances to tantalise spectators and shift their perception of what a mobile could be. His words were important, as was watching a simple gesture activate an application or switch screen views. The demonstration of what his words meant completed the seduction. The Apple demonstrations paved the groundwork for existing assumptions about technology to be transformed. I was performing the same thing, but in the opposite direction. There were numerous examples that demonstrate the capabilities of technology. I was gathering instances to demonstrate the limitations. My collection of failed demos served as a counterweight to the celebrations of technical progress. The white mask failure I documented was an example of a counter-demo. But, exactly, what is a counter-demo? I was offering a counternarrative to the research and accompanying headlines lauding breakthroughs in computer vision in the case of the white mask. I chose to record screencasts for "AI, Ain't I A

Woman?" to generate counter-demos. These experiments challenged the alleged sophistication of AI systems that were eagerly promoted. If these companies' commercially offered items were sold to a large market, I felt they would perform quite well on most people's faces. At the time, these companies provided publicly available online demos of their AI product capabilities, so anyone with some time, an internet connection, and a photo could upload an image and observe how the demos worked. I screen recorded my visits to these websites and suffered through loading animations of revolving wheels that preceded the display of results to create counter-demos. Some incorporated coloured boxes to help pinpoint a head in a picture. All of them included some sort of description of what the uploaded photographs featured. When I uploaded a photo of Sojourner Truth to Google, it returned the title "gentleman." Truth had struggled to be treated on equal footing with a gentleman, but she was also outspoken about the fact that she, too, was a woman. My spoken word algorithmic audit was named after her famous 1851 "Ain't I a Woman?" speech. Truth was also in the business of dismantling dangerous narratives by sharing counter-demos to wide audiences.

THE DAGUERREOTYPE was the first publicly available and widely used photographic technique in the 1840s. Given the scientific instruments used to create images, the daguerreotype was considered to be objective, similar to how some may perceive artificial intelligence today. Photography, on the other hand, can be utilised in the service of harmful undertakings that masquerade as scientific impartiality. Louis Agassiz's slave daguerreotypes were created to investigate differences between "African blacks" and "European whites" in order to "scientifically" prove his notion of white superiority. His daguerreotypes stressed phenotypic differences to imply that there were numerous species of humans, allowing for a racial hierarchy that favoured white Europeans. These "scientific" studies' demeaning portrayal of entirely nude enslaved folks complemented the continuous cultural and political denigration of Black people in the United States, justifying and naturalising their subjection and brutalization. Sojourner Truth, aware of the power of images and the stories they may convey, used photography to portray herself in the dress code associated with middle-class white women of the time. I submitted this image of Truth, dressed in what was supposed to be fundamentally feminine clothing, to Google's system—and Google branded it "gentleman."

In her "Ain't I A Woman?" speech, Sojourner Truth became a powerful orator who pushed for abolition and women's rights while also pointing out discrepancies in the reasoning used by white women to support these rights. She used her voice to advocate for change, but she also utilised her image to make money by selling cartes de visite (collectible cards with images and messages that were popular in the 1860s as a means of mass communication). Truth's photos not only gave financial support, but also advocated for the abolition of slavery, joining the ongoing endeavour of utilising photography to show Black people in dignified ways. Her photos were her counter-demonstrations.

In her mission, she was not alone. With daguerreotypes, Frederick Douglass harnessed the power of photography to tell a different story than Agassiz's slave daguerreotypes. Douglass became the most photographed person of the nineteenth century, and he used dignified portraits of himself using daguerreotypes and other photography techniques to humanise Black people for the wider public while advocating for abolition.

Truth and Douglass expertly used prominent technology to shatter dehumanising portrayals created with the same instruments. They demonstrated that counter-demonstrations do more than just demonstrate; they also demolish assumptions by providing real-world experiences that upset the existing quo. Similarly, AI systems can be utilised as both oppressive and liberating instruments. Through counter-demo, I question the premise of the tech demo as a performance that encourages the use of technology. The critique of artificial intelligence, like Sojourner Truth's critique of white women's marginalisation of the perspectives and experiences of women of colour—a critique that strengthens the impact of the women's rights movement—is not a Luddite call to break machines, but a call to break harmful assumptions about machines, allowing the construction of better tools and, more importantly, better societies.

After recording the counter-demos of truth and other important women, I collaborated with the Ford Foundation to create a video poem that coupled the counter-demos with verse, resulting in the first algorithmic audit given as a spoken word poem. "AI, Ain't I A Woman?" expanded from performance metrics to performance arts, building on the algorithmic audit that comprised the "Gender Shades" research. I was more confident in calling myself a code poet, and I followed in the footsteps of Truth and Douglass by creating a counter-demo to combat negative racial assumptions. They used photography to challenge damaging ideas about the dignity of enslaved people. I utilised my counter-demos to challenge preconceptions about AI's neutrality. I am not alone in using counter-demo to demonstrate technological constraints. In 2009, YouTube user wzamen01 shared a viral video of an HP laptop with face tracking capabilities. At the time of writing, the video has over 3 million views and over 65 hundred comments. The video application displayed was intended to pan with the movement of the face in the video feed. While the system functioned perfectly for the person with lighter complexion in the frame referred to as "Wanda," the pan feature did not operate for the person with darker skin. "I'm Black," the individual known as "Desi" says. "I believe my darkness is interfering with the computer's ability to track me." Despite the deep learning breakthrough and consistent reports of technical improvement in the performance of facial recognition systems, Black faces still shattered the frame seven years later when I donned a white mask. In response to public scrutiny and condemnation of unpleasant and insulting labels used in the dataset's "person" category, around 600,000 photos were identified to be removed from ImageNet, one of the most significant computer vision datasets, in September 2019. ImageNet Roulette, a now-retired interactive application developed by artist Trevor Paglen and scholar Kate Crawford as part of the Training Humans project, catalysed significant public awareness. Anyone with access to the ImageNet Roulette website could contribute an image and have it categorised by a deep neural network trained on images from the ImageNet dataset. Some of the outcomes were shocking, including counter-demonstrations in which a dark-skinned guy was dubbed "wrongdoer, offender," an Asian woman was labelled "jihadist," and others. The hashtag #imagenet roulette quickly became popular. The website served as a participatory evocative audit, allowing users to witness directly the representational problems created by an algorithmic system. This work shows how a strategically placed emotive audit can result in real-world change. An army of people who have been harmed by algorithms has destroyed complacency, questioned the prevalent rhetoric on machine neutrality, and increased the push to resist algorithmic damages. Each social media post with the hashtags displaying objectionable labels increased pressure on the ImageNet dataset's creators to respond, especially as news coverage about the viral hashtag grew. The project's contribution was not just in modifying ImageNet, but also in raising awareness of the dangers of building and implementing algorithmic systems targeted at identifying humans. Frederick douglass reminisces that the stories we tell through imagery can empower those whose authority is not based on great financial resources:

Poets, prophets, and reformers are all picture-makers, and this capacity is the key to their power and success. They view what ought to be through the lens of what is, and they work to eliminate the contradiction. As a code poet, I use words, performance, video, and technical research to highlight the contradictions between the promises we hear about technology, such as artificial intelligence advancing humanity, and the reality I and others witness when technology oppresses rather than liberates. Along the lines of "AI, Ain't I A Woman?" I attempted to construct a piece that combined the performance metrics of the "Gender Shades" algorithmic audit with performance art in order to viscerally explain the implications of the findings, which revealed that for all systems, women of colour perform the lowest. In the luxury of my computer screen, I let the poet take centre stage. The true test was approaching. What reaction might other researchers and decision-makers have to this poetic risk? Will my research be taken seriously? I was anxious that the subjectivity of my poetry would be contrasted with the objectivity of my technological studies. If it appeared that I already had a conclusion in mind before acquiring and assessing the facts, I would be perceived as prejudiced and so less believable. My job as an AI researcher was on the line.

CHAPTER 12
POET VS. GOLIATH IN THE WILD

As prime ministers, presidents, top-ranking government officials, and a code poet visited Davos, snipers positioned on rooftops and the airspace over the city was cleared. I had a sneaking suspicion that the snipers were not there to protect me. It was January 2019, and I was no longer in my research lab. Just like I felt living at the corner of Bow and Arrow streets as a resident tutor at Harvard, I felt at the intersection of privilege and injustice in this location. In the same way that I stood out against the spotless white walls of the Media Lab, I stood out against the white-encased landscape of the Swiss Alps in winter. Months before, I was invited to discuss my findings at the World Economic Forum (WEF), an annual gathering of political, business, cultural, and other leaders aimed at setting global and sector agendas. I was hesitant to go, and not just because of the harsh weather. The international Economic Forum was a symbol of globalisation and free trade, which further centralised international power in the hands of the Global North and corporations. I sought counsel from Ethan, who had been named a WEF Young Global Leader a decade before. The appeal of having access to prominent decision-makers could not be denied. There were, however, other power dynamics to consider. Was my participation really going to make a difference, or was it just for show? Finally, Ethan emphasised that talking just to those who agree with you will not result in change. He warned me to temper my expectations because there were several levels of access. Finally, he provided me with advice on how to use the Swiss public transit system and that I acquired a larger coat. I proceeded to the registration area, wrapped in a red oversized coat, and received a white badge with my face printed on it. I walked down a covered tunnel, past armed guards. I was directed to a container containing an odd item of conference swag: attachable snow spikes for shoes, as long as I had the proper access credentials. Broken ankles were apparently prevalent among the unprepared, so I purchased three sets. I wasn't going to take a chance on the ice roadways. I wandered around the facility looking for the location where I would be presenting my findings and screening my video poem. As I navigated perilous ice patches, often disoriented and feeling out of place, it became evident that I was not a member of the WEF's inner circle. When a guard lunged for a rifle as a companion attempted to drop me off at a hotel for designated badge holders, I was reminded that my presence in some areas was the exception rather than the rule. A pleasant figure screamed my name and waved heartily as I drove there. Professor Cynthia Breazeal was among those bringing MIT President Rafael Reif to the forum. She informed me about her first time attending and provided me with some advice on how to make the most of my visit. I felt grateful and encouraged to be following in her footsteps once more. When I began my art project as a master's student, I had no idea the fallout would lead me to a platform in Switzerland discussing the flaws of AI as world leaders discussed how to employ AI in what was being referred to as the fourth industrial revolution. I wasn't sure where I belonged. Was I the one issuing the warnings? Was I the young scholar offering technical insights to provide businesses a competitive advantage? Was I supposed to deliver provocative words and entertainment as the poet? I was eager to return home after overcoming my initial pre-talk nerves and completing my presentation, but I left the audience with a teaser. "In just a few days, I will be publishing another research paper as a follow-up to 'Gender Shades.'" It includes findings from all of the corporations mentioned here as well as another IT behemoth. "Keep an eye on this!"

That evening, I attended an MIT reception. I saw President Reif fundraising there. I wasn't used to seeing folks at the top of the food chain in my environment requesting help. I knew intellectually that one of the duties of a university president was to generate funds, but I had never seen or heard it done in person. "These are the rooms where it happens," I reasoned. I realised that my duty in this arena was to be a spokesperson of why contributing to MIT was a worthwhile investment. Was I a one-trick pony? I was asked to another MIT event the next day, but I had other commitments. I was liberated. I decided to be the life of the party. An elegant pair of piano-black dress shoes and another pair of tennis shoes proclaimed the arrival of two travel companions who were here to celebrate my twenty-ninth birthday. They'd shot images of themselves in swimsuits holding Happy Birthday signs while standing in the snow on the back porch, framing the zigzagging mountain panorama. I made a wish as I blew out the candles on a rainbow-beamed cake. "Give me love, grace, and safety." "Please let me be a vessel for change."

Ethan and Megan had recommended me to use my time in Switzerland to make connections. I had other plans. I decided to take the entire day off to celebrate my birthday and make memories in the snow with my pals. We began by taking snowboarding lessons. Aside from the vacant airspace over Davos, the ski slopes were mostly deserted. According to our skiing instructor, many locals fled Davos during the World Economic Forum to take advantage of the extra rental revenue and peace and quiet away from the surge of visitors. He carefully guided us down the practice hill before urging us to board the ski lift and test our wobbly basic skills on the way down the mountain. As a former skateboarder, I was humbled every time I found myself sitting on a snow throne. I eventually found myself in a stopping flow, gathering up speed and sliding and slipping down the pure white-powdered mountain. My overconfidence in my snowboarding talents, given my earlier skateboarding expertise, was similar to how some tech companies were releasing AI technologies. Success in one field does not imply success in another. Attempting to snowboard with skateboarding methods hurt both my pride and my bottom. Launching immature and inappropriate goods has a long-term impact on the bottom line of technology organisations. Using skewed datasets or depending on assumptions that require ideal conditions increases the likelihood of failure. Skateboarding and snowboarding teach lessons in artificial intelligence development. Snowboarding on a practice slope, like having an AI system learn on training data, is helpful, but it does not entirely prepare you for traversing harder terrain. And, as with skateboarding, you might begin learning at a park with obstacles and ramps that are thoughtfully spaced apart, but that experience does not fully prepare you for street skating, which in my case meant navigating suburban sidewalks with features like pebbles, sidewalk cracks, and potholes that were not designed for skating. Bruises soon followed. AI technologies that have shown promise in creating efficiency, such as optimising energy use in data centres, are appealing for application in other sectors. DeepMind was acquired by Google and proven effective in saving the corporation 40% on data centre cooling costs by applying AI to optimise energy efficiency. Working in a reasonably limited setting is not the same as working in an uncontrolled environment. Early face detection researchers quickly discovered that training data from people photographed in well-lit environments with set poses did not equip systems for unconstrained environments, also known as the real world, where most people do not walk around with studio-quality lighting. When researchers began gathering photographs of faces "in the wild," candid images of people posted online to improve face identification systems, it was analogous to transitioning from a good indoor skate park with a beginner's area to the streets to negotiate real-world conditions. Mountain snowboarding uses multiple ratings to indicate the difficulty and risk of various routes. Beginners should not attempt to navigate Double Black Diamond routes reserved for individuals with not just confidence but also experience. Applying AI systems to high-stakes scenarios that have not been tested on a diverse variety of individuals or settings is akin to a newbie confidently ascending a Black Diamond route without first understanding the basics and without the right equipment. We still lived in a world where law enforcement might use AI systems that had not been properly vetted for accuracy to inform investigative leads when I was snowboarding in Davos that January. As we saw in the situations of Robert Williams, Michael Oliver, and Nijeer Parks, false arrests followed. All of these Black guys were detained as a result of a facial recognition error. While I was navigating the WEF, I was mentally prepared for another event. Deborah Raji wanted to work on a research paper during her internship with me, in addition to the Black Panther Face Scorecard. We decided to repeat the "Gender Shades" report and see how companies fared a year later—and to include two new companies. She suggested we include Clarifai, where she had interned. I suggested we include Amazon because they were providing facial recognition technologies to police departments and were the target of many protests. Hundreds of thousands of people and forty civil rights organisations had signed letters urging that Amazon stop selling its Amazon Rekognition tool to law enforcement the previous summer. Given the stakes, law enforcement applications of any emerging technologies were already Black Diamond territory. Using facial recognition technologies that had not even been demonstrated to be fit for the stated purpose, let alone tested outside, was both risky and irresponsible. While I was navigating the WEF, I was mentally prepared for another event. Deborah Raji wanted to work on a research paper during her internship with me, in addition to the Black Panther Face Scorecard. We decided to repeat the "Gender Shades" report and see how companies fared a year later—and to include two new companies. She suggested we include Clarifai, where she had interned. I suggested we include Amazon because they were providing facial recognition technologies to police departments and were the target of many protests. Hundreds of thousands of people and forty civil rights organisations had signed letters urging that Amazon stop selling its Amazon Rekognition tool to law enforcement the previous summer. Given the stakes, law enforcement applications of any emerging technologies were already Black Diamond territory. Using facial recognition technologies that had not even been demonstrated to be fit for the stated purpose, let alone tested outside, was both risky and irresponsible. Deborah, whom I began to refer to as Agent Deb, and I were slated to present our findings at the AAAI Conference on Artificial Intelligence, Ethics, and Society in Honolulu in January 2019—right after the World Economic Forum. The New York Times was supposed to publish an article regarding algorithmic bias discoveries on the top page of the business section the day before the conference. The article's finalisation was a difficult procedure. Amazon staff stated at the last minute that they had not had a chance to review the data, despite the fact that I had documented documentation of sharing this information with the corporation. Perhaps the information was misplaced or was sent to spam. Moreover, the previous summer, I published a public letter to Jeff Bezos containing similar early findings. Amazon could no longer disregard the research findings after a peer-reviewed paper was published alongside a New York Times feature article. Based on Amazon's behind-the-scenes reaction and the time it would take me to go to the AAAI conference from Switzerland, I drafted a Medium piece anticipating Amazon's pushback on my last day in Davos. As I scribbled furiously on my laptop, two thousand words of counterarguments gushed from my fingertips. I emailed the rebuttal article to hundreds of reporters who had previously covered the "Gender Shades" story, informing them that The New York Times was due to publish an article on the new research paper. I informed them that I would be unavailable for comment for the next twenty-four hours due to international travel. There were plenty of quotes in the Medium piece if they wanted them. That, I hoped, would suffice for the time being. I needed to sleep. I arrived in Honolulu wearing snow boots and a large red winter coat, surrounded by Hawaiian shirts, sandals, and leis. The AAAI conference organisers made the wise decision to hold their meeting in a tropical location in January. As much as I adored the snow slopes, Waikiki Beach was a nice respite from the winter chill of Davos and Boston. Deb, my agent, and I met in a hotel lobby. She was scheduled to give a presentation the following day. I requested she give the paper alone because she was the first author. It was unusual to have an undergraduate as the primary author of a study, but I wanted to demonstrate that young researchers could make significant contributions to research. I'd be there to support her, just as Timnit had been for me on the "Gender Shades" paper the previous winter. Agent Deb took me through her first-draft presentation. When she was done, I raised my right brow. "You can't present it like that.... They will laugh at us." She winced slightly. We sat on the floor for a few hours, revising the slides. I was especially harsh on Deb because I knew we would not be spared as young, marginalised researchers up against some of the world's top tech forces. I'd rather be harsh on her now so that we can weather what's to come. Among the things I could teach her, I highlighted that she should learn how to communicate and share research in an engaging manner.

"Many people can learn technical skills." What will set you apart from your colleagues is your ability to communicate and convey a story about your technical work. It is what makes people see why change is required. I don't want to offend your sensibilities. I want you to be prepared for the wind."

The next day, I left my belongings in my seat and wandered around like a happy father shooting photos as Agent Deb presented "Actionable Auditing" to a gathering of roughly 400 people. Francesca Rossi from IBM was present, and I sat with her and a few of her coworkers. In this paper, IBM performed substantially better, whereas Amazon was behind all of its competitors. The "Actionable Auditing" paper was awarded best student paper, and I put down my camera to pose with Deb for the official conference photographer.

Deb's first research article, for which she was the first author, had won an award as well as a financial reward. We also had photographs published in the New York Times piece "Amazon Is Pushing Facial Technology That a Study Says Could Be Biassed," written by Natasha Singer. "I cannot pay like a tech start-up, but what I can teach you will set you up to go beyond me," I promised Agent Deb when she joined me. Learn from everyone and strive to be better."

THEN THE ATTACKS BEGAN. Dr. Matt Wood, an Amazon vice president, stated our research and the New York Times article were "misleading" and drew "false conclusions." The topic Hal had brought up years before resurfaced. Wood stated that because our work focused on the gender classification feature of Amazon Rekognition, the results did not extend to the product's facial recognition capabilities. I thought I was clear when I said that the study's findings raised worries about other face-to-face tasks. Did they truly fail to perceive the connection? Unlike IBM's reaction, which made me believe that change was possible, Amazon's attitude made me question the extent to which giant organisations could be trusted.

Amazon and Microsoft were competing for a $10 billion deal to deliver AI services to the Pentagon at the time. It was not a good time to have your AI talents called into doubt. Amazon's counterattacks persisted, and I responded with a second Medium essay. I felt like I was facing the Goliath known as Amazon alone in the wilderness. None of the other businesses had taken a hostile stance. I questioned if I had gone too far in my study by confronting Amazon. I was concerned that I had put Agent Deb—an undergraduate with plans to go graduate school—in too much danger. Prospective computer science departments may view her as too risky. Potential employers in the IT field may blacklist her. As the strikes intensified, she inquired what she could do to assist. "Leave this to me. Concentrate on your studies." I kept her in the dark while I planned my next move.

As the Amazon hack unfolded, I was encouraged to see organisations such as the American Civil Liberties Union of Massachusetts and the Georgetown Law Center on Privacy and Technology come to our aid. They took to Twitter to express their support for both the research and for me personally. More was required. I was concerned that if other researchers saw what Amazon was doing to us and no academics came up to defend us, other researchers would view the professional danger of this type of research as too great. The response of the research community to Amazon's attack on "Actionable Auditing" would set a precedent. I expressed my worries to Timnit and Meg Mitchell. They were the co-leaders of the Google AI Ethics team at the time and had the authority to speak out. They organised a statement signed by 75 researchers expressing their support for our research. Professor Anima Anandkumar, the former lead AI scientist at Amazon, and Professor Yoshua Bengio, a Turing Prize winner (think of it as a Nobel Prize for computer science), were among the signatories. Given how much research funding Amazon provides, all of these computer science researchers faced major professional risks by advocating for the project. Bloomberg published a story titled "Amazon Schooled on AI Facial Technology by Turing Prize Winner." Yoshua summed up the researchers' letter when he claimed Amazon's response to the study was "disappointing." "It is also important to have social and scholarly debates about what is socially and ethically acceptable in the use of these new technologies," he added. This case illustrates such issues very clearly and is an excellent method to raise public awareness." I was appreciative for the help I received from people outside of my host institution.

Shortly after the release of the "Actionable Auditing" report, Amazon stated that it will collaborate with the National Science Foundation (NSF) to fund the Program on Fairness in Artificial Intelligence, which Amazon had openly criticised. In an op-ed for Nature, Yochai Benkler remarked that when the NSF validates Amazon's procedure for a $7.6-million program (0.03% of Amazon's 2018 R&D spending), it undermines the role of public research as a counterweight to industry-funded research. When a university takes funding from a company to examine the moral, political, and legal ramifications of behaviours integral to that company's economic model, it relinquishes its central position. Governments that transfer policy frameworks to industry-dominated bodies suffer the same fate. Yes, institutions have put in place some precautions. The NSF will award research grants using its standard peer-review method, with or without Amazon's assistance, but Amazon will retain the contractual, technical, and organisational resources to push projects that meet its objectives.

I concurred. I also noted that the majority of the public support I received came from outside of MIT and the Media Lab. I was especially thankful to Kade Crockford of the American Civil Liberties Union of Massachusetts and Alvaro Bedoya of the Georgetown Law Center on Privacy and Technology for publicly defending my work on social media. "I need backup!" I said to Ethan. I'm competing with Amazon."

Ethan jumped into action and published a piece defending my work. Others I contacted could not openly support me for a variety of reasons. They were primarily concerned with either funding or antagonising a firm as powerful as Amazon. At that point, I felt basically abandoned by the majority of MIT leadership. When "Gender Shades" received great public attention, there was no hesitancy in standing alongside me in the sun. Would they still support me in the face of bad attention? I was witnessing Amazon's power firsthand. Amazon provided funding for important research programs, and MIT and the Media Lab were actively fundraising. This was perhaps not the best time to ruffle feathers.

I excitedly contacted my parents in December of 2019. "I've been vindicated by the feds!" The National Institute of Standards and Technology (NIST) had finally published a long-awaited article on the impact of race, age, and gender on the performance of facial recognition software. "For one-to-one matching [facial verification], the team saw higher rates of false positives for Asian and African American faces relative to images of Caucasians," according to the government website. The differentials frequently ranged from 10 to 100 times, depending on the algorithm." I was startled to see that the difference in accuracy between Asian and African American faces and Caucasian faces could be up to 100 times greater. "For one-to-many matching [facial identification], the team saw higher rates of false positives for African American females," the findings revealed. False positive differentials in one-to-many matching are especially relevant since the repercussions could include false accusations." So, while Amazon was correct that my studies focused on gender classification rather than facial verification or identification, I was correct in asserting that the bias observed in my studies was cause for concern in other areas, given the shared technical approaches used with a variety of facial recognition technologies. Amazon, unlike Microsoft, did not submit its systems to be evaluated for this historic study in 2019. My illusion of safety had already dissipated by the time NIST's vindication arrived in December. I assumed that based on my work at an academic institution such as MIT would provide me with backup and support if my work was disputed. I expected the Media Lab, which promoted my work to attract students and media attention, would protect me. It was disheartening to feel as if I had to beg for safety just to receive very little. I was even more eager to get out of the lab whenever possible. But, if I couldn't speak truth to power at the university, where could I go? Who would be on my side, and with whom could I form an alliance?

CHAPTER 13
BROOKLYN TENANTS

I felt unanchored several months after I left Hawaii with Agent Deb and did everything I could to defend my study. There was something missing. The discussion of the hazards of facial recognition technologies and AI damages was only the beginning. This work was more than just theory or study. There was more to the job than just speaking with tech companies. Yes, organisations have to modify their approach to developing and deploying AI technologies. And those modifications may help to prevent future injury. However, without legislation, there was no certainty that businesses would alter. I wished I could be closer to the ground. I wanted to assist genuine people who were affected by these systems. I wanted to believe that my work was important, not because it was acknowledged by other academics, but because it had a genuine impact on the lives of the excoded.

My chance to connect directly with the excoded arrived in April 2019. When I saw a time-bound request from a Brooklyn lawyer while scrolling through my inbox, I slowed down. I just had a week to react.

26th of April, 2019

Hello there, Joy.

I work at Brooklyn Legal Services in NYC with the Tenant Rights Coalition on a case involving a private residential building owner attempting to implement facial recognition software in place of the current keyless fob system at a major residential building in Brooklyn. Given that the residents of this vast 700+ unit complex are largely people of colour, women, and the elderly, your publication, Gender Shades, raises severe accuracy and bias concerns about the planned system.

We were hoping you could assist us in better understanding the possibility for algorithmic discrimination with the equipment the building owner has proposed installing here. StoneLock created the facial recognition program, which uses a heatmap of a person's face to grant access. They say that it does not distinguish between gender, sex, or skin colour because it "merely reads data points on a person's face and assigns a number." I believe our most fundamental question is, can the suggested facial recognition system still discriminate based on demographic and phenotypic factors despite the fact that it uses heatmap technology rather than video-surveillance facial identification? We are perplexed as to how they can promise there is no risk of algorithmic discrimination since zero validation studies on the accuracy/bias of this specific system exist. I've included copies of a marketing handout and a paper that the building owner supplied with us detailing the intended entry mechanism. Any ideas or insights would be much appreciated. Also, this is a bit of an emergency. Because the tenants live in a rent-stabilised building, the landlord must obtain permission from the state body that monitors rent-stabilisation regulations in New York before replacing the current entrance system. We're working with the tenants to register an opposition with the state agency by next Wednesday, 5/1, and would appreciate it if you could share any technical information with us as soon as possible so that we may reinforce our argument against the owner's proposal. I eagerly await your response!

They were drafting a statement in opposition to a landlord's request to install a facial recognition entry system at the Atlantic Towers housing complex. After a preliminary call, I studied their docs and provided some short feedback on the sections that I understood, aside from the legalese. As I was boarding a flight to North Carolina to visit friends, I received a phone call from the lawyer to discuss my input. More calls came in as she rushed to meet her deadline, and she received a second request.

"I hope this is a good time to call."

"I'm in the airport, but we should have a little time."

"Would you be willing to work on an amicus letter of support for us?"

"Uh, I will need some time to think about it."

I needed some time to research what an amicus letter of support was, and I had to decide whether I had any business writing one. I was deviating from traditional graduate student work by spending less time at the Media Lab and more time on trains and flights to present my research findings. Foodcam photographs of leftovers in my email inbox were becoming the only thing that reminded me that I was still in school. My PhD coursework was complete, and my supervisor was relatively hands-off. I took full advantage of the situation. I felt free to explore, just like my first year as a master's student. Rather than focusing on publishing more papers from my thesis work, I focused on reaching out to people outside of academia. "AI, Ain't I A Woman?" was featured in a number of art shows throughout the world. I'd even delivered the white mask that started this adventure as part of a five-year touring art exhibition curated by London's Barbican Centre, which opens on May 16. The amicus brief was due on May 12. On May 22, I was also called to provide expert testimony at a congressional hearing. I had plenty of time and plenty of motivation. I started with the amicus letter. I began working on a statement after examining StoneLock's marketing materials and the tenants' opposing statement, which was supported by the coalition. Each public statement issued by AJL served two purposes: one, to express support or opposition to specific acts, and two, to educate others who were thinking about adopting or opposing a similar system. I was ecstatic to be able to immediately apply my studies and skills to help the tenants. Hal's rhetorical queries regarding the importance of this effort no longer troubled me. I saw directly how it gave those experiencing real-world hardships hope. The nagging desire to always prove myself began to fade as well. It didn't matter if the research was presented at an academic conference or featured in The New York Times. It was significant because it might be utilised to effect tangible change in the lives of ordinary people. To further the cause, I used StoneLock's own materials to emphasise the importance of security system users supporting the system. Security professionals realise that systems that are transparent to the user have a distinct edge over those that cause discomfort or aggravation. The truth is that conscious and unconscious user adoption and compliance are critical to the success of any security solution.— StoneLock.

In the opposing letter, 134 tenants at Atlantic Towers expressed serious dissatisfaction with the StoneLock system. They had every right to be concerned about the system's accuracy, consent, data breaches and exploitation, and security dangers. They were concerned that algorithmic prejudice might cause the system to fail on them, making it difficult to access their property without further complications. When they moved into the residences, they had not explicitly agreed to have their faces used for a biometric entrance system. They had no guarantees that their facial data would not be sold and used for other reasons, or turned over to the authorities. I supplied data and pertinent instances in the amicus letter to back up what the tenants were already claiming. StoneLock's marketing brochures didn't include anything about how their method worked on different types of faces. This was especially troubling given that more than 90% of the tenants were individuals of colour. They were mostly female-identified, and they included both minors and the elderly. The vast majority of the tenants belonged to one or more of the categories with the highest failure rates in U.S. government-sponsored research on the accuracy of facial recognition technology that I reviewed.

StoneLock claimed that their solution had been tested in 40% of Fortune 100 businesses. I was sceptical that the company demographics matched those of the renters at Atlantic Towers. The practice of testing systems in one setting and then transporting them to another invites context collapse. The actual world is more challenging than relying on first tests in one environment to support deployment in another. I remember hearing Kate Crawford say, "Caribou are not kangaroos." She remarked during an AI Now event at the Media Lab that self-driving car systems trained in a location where caribou crossed the road would be unprepared for Australia, where kangaroos crossed the road instead of caribou. When a kangaroo hops, a system expecting the animal to proceed straight across the street may mistakenly pump the gas and collide with the kangaroo on its way down. Employees of Fortune 100 companies are not tenants of Atlantic Towers.

Another case of context collapse happened when Winterlight Labs, a Canadian start-up, developed a system that employed machine learning to detect Alzheimer's disease symptoms in voice recordings. Their algorithm had been trained on first-language English-speaking Canadians. The algorithm did not match the training data when tested on Canadians who spoke French as their first language. Because the indicators used to infer Alzheimer's disease may also overlap with signals communicated by someone searching for the proper term or stringing together words in odd ways in a second language, the context collapse happened.

When I visited with Tranae Moran and Icemae, two long-term tenants at Atlantic Towers, they had a lot of data questions. We sat at a picnic table between two skyscrapers. She said, "How do we know they aren't giving our data to the police?" with the question "Can't our data be hacked?" "If they are keeping my face data, shouldn't I get some money?" Tranae wondered. with the question "Is our face data useless like they claim?" Their inquiries indicated that those affected by algorithmic decision-making were far from uninterested once they were made aware of the risks. These women reminded me of the personal consequences of algorithmic harms. The work went much beyond a research project. The responsibility I felt to assist grew heavier. What began as a graduate art project is now being used to depict failed deployments of facial recognition systems.

Both Tranae and Icemae were correct. Tech companies' ongoing efforts to collect more diverse datasets reveal that their data as Black women was in high demand. While working on the "AI: More Than Human" Barbican art installation, I saw another space with a shortage of different data. Deepfakes were becoming more common. The use of generative adversarial networks (GANs) enabled the development of photorealistic artificial faces. Nonetheless, these phoney humans were seeded by a training image dataset. And, like with all machine learning algorithms, data determines fate. The curators of the exhibition sought to show photos of people from the Pilot Parliaments dataset. However, the EU's new General Data Protection Regulation included a provision requiring agreement for the dissemination of biometric data. I didn't want to take any chances because the dataset included the faces of EU citizens in the form of Icelandic, Finnish, and Swedish parliament members. I told the Barbican about my reservations.

The exhibition team stated that they could only present the faces of Africans in the dataset. Even though there were no laws safeguarding African people, I opposed it because I did not want them to have fewer protections. They proposed utilising a deep fake face generator to represent the dataset as a solution. I alluded to the fact that "these systems are likely trained on skewed data, so I suspect the image of those meant to represent Africans might not look quite as realistic as others." They went for it regardless. When I analysed the datasets, the lighter-skinned deep fakes appeared to be convincing humans, whereas the darker-skinned ones contained numerous examples that did not pass muster as a photorealistic portrayal. The hairlines and texture were unnatural—and not in a nice way.

The faces that dominated the most frequent publicly available face datasets at the time were not those of the elderly and primarily Black and Brown tenants. Furthermore, the demographic and phenotypic makeup of the StoneLock proprietary system's training set was unknown. The corporation simply asked us to trust their word without demonstrating how the system was trained. When it comes to artificial intelligence systems, confidence must be earned rather than assumed. Tranae and Iceman had every reason to be anxious about cops accessing their data. In 2019, there was no formal federal law addressing the use of facial recognition technologies, putting residents at risk of serious harm. There was no formal regulation governing law enforcement or government use of facial recognition technology. Access to the system's valuable store of biometric data connected to personally identifiable information could be sought by law enforcement and even government agencies such as the FBI and ICE. This access may expose an already vulnerable community to harassment and worse. Such an arrangement would expose residents to police profiling and false accusations, as well as further data exploitation and privacy violations.

Furthermore, while StoneLock claims that near-infrared light can outperform other systems in terms of accuracy, they do not address the special issues of near-infrared facial recognition. For example, the accuracy of near-infrared facial recognition may be altered by the individual's mental and physical state, which can be influenced by illness, alcohol, or exercise. StoneLock's corporate training grounds, workplace locations where alcohol consumption is restricted if not prohibited, and which employees tend not to frequent while ill, may be unsuitable for the variety presented in a residential community. StoneLock also claimed that their technology was free of bias due to the type of imaging they used. However, they lacked sufficient data to back up this allegation. Instead, they claimed that the infrared technology they were employing protected them from the risks associated with other facial recognition systems.

WHILE I COULD NOT DIRECTLY influence the activities security and tech businesses made to develop facial recognition systems, I could and did focus my efforts on equipping others. Educating people on the front lines of the struggle for algorithmic justice was another critical function I envisaged for AJL.

The "Gender Shades" research has been incorporated into successful efforts to push for legislation that restricts the use of facial recognition technology by government agencies, including police departments, in addition to being used directly by impacted communities to resist algorithmic harms at a local level. After the study was published, Matt Cagle and Jacob Snow of the ACLU of Northern California were inspired to conduct an algorithmic audit of Amazon Rekognition. The ACLU audit that followed the "Gender Shades" design targeted elected officials. Instead of international legislatures, the ACLU audit concentrated on the United States House of Representatives. The goal of the "Gender Shades"-inspired audit was to raise public awareness about police use of facial recognition technology and persuade legislators to pass laws. In their audit, twenty-eight members of Congress were mistakenly linked with mugshots.

Furthermore, campaign materials prepared in support of limiting police use of facial recognition cited the "Gender Shades" study as evidence for real concerns, such as the fact that these tools compound pre-existing racial bias. On May 14, 2019, San Francisco became the first city to prohibit police officers from using facial recognition technology. The ACLU of Massachusetts has also spearheaded successful legislative initiatives in collaboration with a number of organisations, resulting in Massachusetts having the most municipal limits on government use of face recognition as of this writing. The findings of the "Gender Shades" study were also integrated into the Massachusetts campaign activities. I was both delighted and taken aback by the scope and effect of the work.

These experiences taught me the value of group action and the importance of taking time away from the lab. The criticisms of my work that pointed out how it may be exploited by businesses to shore up flaws in their AI systems are correct. The concentration on classification accuracy in "Gender Shades" can improve state authority by reifying control categories and providing insights into areas where control can be subverted, allowing the state to deliberate on how to limit or fight subversion. Simultaneously, substantial classification failures using contestable labels show how fragile AI systems—even those built by major companies—can be. Such flaws call into question simple assumptions about machine neutrality and technical objectivity.

The same work was also used to support bans and moratoriums on detrimental applications of facial recognition technologies. Because these technologies were already under development, keeping my results hidden would not have avoided harm. My speaking out gave me the opportunity to evaluate other options, including nonuse. This was the case with San Francisco's ban on police enforcement using facial recognition technology. After the success of "AI, Ain't I A Woman?" Google ceased using gendered labelling in its commercial AI systems, demonstrating how bias awareness may lead to changes in a company's design practices. Gender identifiers such as "gentleman" were not required to be utilised in their automated labelling at all. Other firms began using less precise explanations of their work, such as "perceived gender" rather than "gender" in characterising the types of labels produced by their systems. I'm more certain than ever of Audre Lorde's words, "Your silence will not protect you." Despite the conflicting reactions to my work, I am glad I stood up. However, the movement required — and continues to require — more people inside and outside of labs to speak up when they encounter damaging AI systems. When we see a lack of representation in datasets, we need AI practitioners to use their position to document the concerns and ensure that the limitations of a system or study findings are communicated alongside the hopeful prospects. To prevent harm, we need people who are willing to stop product releases or change the design of a system.

We need artists to employ their imagination to create evocative works that humanise the impact of AI-driven errors. We need tenants who will speak out against the installation of intrusive systems and take the initiative to learn more about the technology that we are frequently pushed to adopt without inquiry. We need researchers who take the effort to make their findings accessible and digestible so that the general public understands what is at stake and advocacy groups can pick up the slack to support effective campaigns. We must also recognize the dangers of speaking up against powerful entities. I was generally sheltered from direct dangers in the early days of my profession. When my study was challenged by a tech titan, those days were over. We needed a check on corporate power.

CHAPTER 14
TESTIFY

"Thank you, Chairman Cummings." Max, Megan Smith's black-and-white cat, caught my eye. He appeared uninterested but participated in my practice run before my first congressional hearing. As he unfurled at the swimming pool, Max was intent on licking his right paw. By May 2019, I was growing dissatisfied with academia and more eager to meet with people hurt by AI systems. Nonetheless, I had additional academic hurdles to clear. I needed to complete my general exams, which were a set of tests administered by my committee to assess my knowledge of my field of study. Written take-home assignments were included in the tests. But I was rarely at home these days, as my study provided me opportunities to participate in art shows and speak at conferences all over the world. When the House Committee on Oversight and Reform invited me to testify at a congressional hearing, I was eager to try my hand at persuading policymakers to prevent AI problems. It wasn't just a matter of turning up to answer questions during the hearing; I also had to submit written testimony ahead of time. How was I going to cram for three general exams while still preparing for this hearing? My overflowing email, unfinished meals, and constant weariness were all signs of imminent burnout. I contacted Ethan to see whether my real-world written testimony may serve as a substitute for one of my general exams. Despite my disappointing graduate school experiences, I couldn't dispute the level of flexibility and freedom I had as Ethan's student. He concurred. In 2018, Ethan introduced me to the Ford Foundation, which became the first institution to finance the Algorithmic Justice League in May 2019. My energy was rekindled by the Ford Foundation grant and the reduction in my workload. AJL was no longer just an idea, and I was no longer just a student. Back by the pool, I was fine-tuning the language of my opening statement and soliciting comments from Megan as we lounged in her backyard at the Embassy of Innovation. "Keep it bipartisan," she recommended. "Make sure everyone on the committee understands how it impacts their constituents." I was finishing up my written testimony on my journey from Boston to Washington, DC, which had to be submitted ahead of the first of a series of hearings on face recognition technology. There was still time to prepare my opening five-minute statement 24 hours before the hearing. Earlier that day, I had attended a moot hearing at Georgetown organised by Alvaro Bedoya and Laura Moy. Alvaro stated that a moot hearing was the jargon for a mock hearing. We were in a rearranged conference room with two rows of tables facing each other. The interrogators sat at one table, while the witnesses sat at the other. I looked over at my co-witness, who appeared composed and prepared. The practice round had not gone well for me. The first question Alvaro posed to me proved to be a roadblock. I stumbled through an unsatisfying response and wondered why I was giving congressional testimony. My face became heated. I rarely blushed, but I was purple today. The stakes were quite high: This hearing could drive the federal government to pass much-needed face recognition legislation. Alvaro informed me that the questions he asked during the mock hearing would most likely be much more difficult than anything I would face during the actual hearing. "It will only be broadcast on C-SPAN," I assured myself. "Who watches C-SPAN?" Then Ethan texted me: The Media Lab was hosting a watching party in the atrium on the third level. Alvaro's encouraging words did not deter me from poring over my notes for hours, anticipating questions on the theme "Facial Recognition Technology and Its Impact on Civil Rights and Liberties." I printed out around twenty pages of notes and went over them whenever I had time. The tension was rising. I'd be testifying alongside Neema Singh Guliani, senior legislative counsel for the American Civil Liberties Union; Clare Garvie, coauthor of "The Perpetual Line-Up," a report that inspired me to investigate algorithmic bias; Andrew G. Ferguson, a law professor; and Dr. Cedric Alexander, former president of the National Organization of Black Law Enforcement Executives. Neema was a regular at congressional hearings, and her replies were sharp and concise, with an air of "I said what I said" confidence. To avoid embarrassment, I inquired about the right approach to address the committee members and other basic questions. At the very least, I understood what a moot hearing was. Maybe I'd been too close to the sun, but it was too late to turn around now. If I was going to perish in flames, I wanted to do so in style. My outfit was ready: a crimson blazer, white-rimmed spectacles, a braided faux hawk, and a bracelet inspired by the Wakanda kimoyo beads seen in the film

Black Panther. One thing was certain: I would need magical abilities to go through the next day with my dignity intact.

On May 22, 2019, at 7:00 a.m., I awoke in the Embassy of Innovation's playroom. I knelt next to ancient toys and science experiments. "Please help me, God!" Please give me the words to say. Give me bravery, power, and knowledge." Today was not the day to rely on my own knowledge. The final draft of my opening statement had just been printed downstairs. I hopped down the stairs with Max by my side to join Megan at the kitchen table. In between nibbles of bagels and cream cheese, I practised my remarks. Chairman Elijah Cummings, a Maryland Democrat representing the district that encompasses Baltimore, opened the congressional hearing at 11:00 a.m. "I can relate to facial recognition mistakes," he stated in his opening remarks. I can't tell you how many people have stopped me, mistaking me for John Lewis. I don't always have the heart to tell them, so I just let them snap a picture." Ranking member Jim Jordan, a Republican from Ohio and ardent Trump supporter, also spoke about the privacy issues of utilising facial recognition. Throughout the session, he would emphasise that these systems were being deployed without the authority of Congress. "How does the FBI get access to this data?" He frowned. We had found a topic that troubled both parties during a very polarised period in American politics, with the 2020 elections looming the following fall. The Democrats were particularly concerned about the civil rights implications and the fact that facial recognition put Black and Brown communities at significantly greater danger of damage. Chairman Cummings spoke on the use of face recognition technology on protestors in Baltimore who attended a march to decry the police killing of Freddie Gray. In addition to discussing police brutality, he mentioned the chilling consequences of using facial recognition at protests, which is a threat to the First Amendment right to free expression. Would you feel free to attend a protest if you knew law enforcement would use face recognition technology to track who showed up?

The Republicans frequently brought up the privacy risks of a Big Brother-like authority watching people's movements. Glenn Grothman, a Republican from Wisconsin, raised an issue that I had not considered. "As we begin to have politically incorrect gathering places, a gun show or something, is it something we should fear that our government will use to identify people who have ideas that are not politically correct?"

Clare Garvie reacted in a commanding tone. "Law enforcement agencies have expressed similar concerns." Back in 2011, when the technology was really taking off, a face recognition working group led by the FBI stated that "face recognition could be used as a form of social control, causing people to alter their public behaviours, leading to self-censorship and inhibition."

A widespread misconception about parliamentarians is that their expertise of technology is, at best, limited. I was pleasantly delighted to discover that the lawmakers and their staff had clearly done their homework during the meeting. I must admit, I was not really paying attention to this technology until I was misdiagnosed last year during the ACLU test of members of Congress, said Democratic Representative Jimmy Gomez of California. And it did pique my interest and curiosity in technology, but it felt wrong deep down in my stomach. I began investigating.... I've had nine meetings with Amazon executives, and we've asked questions of specialists from all walks of life, and my concerns have only grown.... Despite the fact that Amazon had not submitted its product to independent testing, it sold it to police departments.... Do you believe third-party testing is necessary for the safe deployment of facial recognition technology, Ms. Buolamwini?

Was a lawmaker truly interested in third-party testing of AI systems? "Absolutely," I said. "One of the things the Algorithmic Justice League has been doing is really evaluating these firms where we can.... We obviously require third-party testing, and we must also ensure that the National Institute of Standards and Technology's examinations are sufficiently broad."

"Yes, because evaluating on an incorrect or biassed dataset will result in incorrect results," Representative Gomez said before giving back to the chairman.

After a time, I realised that not all of the legislators had come to ask questions. Representatives came and went from the meeting, some lingering long enough to make remarks that would make good sound bites for campaigns, others from overlapping committees. Representatives Alexandria Ocasio-Cortez of New York, Rashida Tlaib of Michigan, and Ayanna Pressley of Massachusetts, three members of the Squad, entered the session halfway through. The Squad represented a new generation of junior members who held progressive, left-wing ideals. Representative Pressley halted during her speech to mention that the Algorithmic Justice League was founded in Cambridge, Massachusetts, a city in her district. She explained to the committee that she had read about the concept of the coded gaze in my recent New York Times op-ed, and then she gave me the floor to explain the phrase to them.

Representative Ocasio-Cortez then posed questions to me. Poet of Code (POC) and AOC were in sync.

"I heard your opening statement, Ms. Buolamwini.... We noticed that various algorithms vary in their effectiveness. "Do they work best on women?"

"No."

"Are they most effective on people of colour?"

"Absolutely not."

"Are they most effective on people of different gender expressions?"

"No, in fact it excludes them."

"Which demographic is it mostly effective on?"

"White men."

"And who are the primary engineers and designers of these algorithms?"

"Definitely, white men."

"So we have a technology that was created and designed by one demographic, that is only mostly effective on that one demographic, and they are trying to sell it and impose it on the entirety of the country?"So we have the pale male dataset being utilised as something universal when it comes to depicting the full spectrum of mankind. "And do you think it could exacerbate the already egregious inequalities in our criminal justice system?"

"It already is."

Chairman Cummings responded matter-of-factly, "How so?"

Turning towards him, I said, without missing a beat. "So right now, because you have the propensity for these systems to misidentify Black individuals or Brown communities more often, and you also have confirmation bias, where if I have been said to be a criminal then I am more targeted."

Our back-and-forth revealed a straightforward fact. The affluent few were designing for the masses with little regard for the negative consequences of their work. The repercussions are still being felt. Misidentification helped by automatic facial recognition led to the arrests of Michael Oliver, Nijeer Parks, Robert Williams, and Randall Reid. Williams was unfairly arrested in front of his two young daughters and detained by authorities for the night. Despite the fact that Williams was subsequently released, the memory of his two young daughters seeing their father detained while neighbours watched on cannot be forgotten. He revealed that he has enrolled his children in treatment. The pain of being wrongly detained is indelible, as is the knowledge that resistance could result in a lethal situation. These are only a few of the incidents we are aware of. I consider the inmate who sent me a desperate letter from behind bars, as well as others we may never hear from or from whom we may never learn that facial recognition technologies played a role in their arrests. The glimmer of optimism was that we were still in the early stages of developing facial recognition technologies and artificial intelligence. Our actions now will have long-term ramifications. Chairman Cummings finished the session by saying, "This is one of the best hearings I have seen in my twenty-three years." You were all quite thorough. "Extremely detailed." "Again, I want to thank all of you for your patience....," he added, looking at the clock, which showed nearly three hours had gone since the hearing began. This meeting has been adjourned." He then banged the gavel down. Then he motioned for me to approach the top of the rows of chairs behind wooden panels that led to his vantage point. When I reached the summit of the congressional Everest, he leaned in and said, "I promise you, Congress will do something about this."

The long hours of testimony had energised the chairman of the oversight committee. He leaned in closer and asked, "Now, what do you recommend we do first?" I was both honoured and astonished that he wanted my opinion. I assumed my duty was done. I recognized that my responsibility was not only to teach, but also to offer tangible, attainable, and meaningful acts. "I paused to consider the least contentious action that could be taken to assist everyone involved in the debate over the future of facial recognition technologies in taking steps to reduce harm."Chairman, we want a starting point. We do not yet have a clear picture of how the federal government or organisations receiving federal funds use facial recognition. At the very least, the committee should undertake a survey to determine where the technology is being used, for what purposes, and whose companies are currently or have previously sold to all government agencies."

"We can get that started."

I therefore argued for something that would require more time while simultaneously emphasising the action that I believed would lessen the most risks and harms for the time being.

"Given all of the risks and threats, I strongly advocate for a moratorium on the use of facial recognition by the government." Let us apply the precautionary approach so that we do not deploy technology where enough investigation and debate have not occurred, and when mistakes are extremely costly." He smiled and shook my hand, adding, "Thank you, Ms. Buolamwini."

I thanked him for the opportunity to share my thoughts. His assistant smiled and rose from her chair. "I, too, am from Ghana." You make us so happy. We'll keep in touch and want to learn more."

I hadn't been flying too close to the sun. As I walked out of the Rayburn Building, I grinned to myself. I was born with the ability to fly with words and testify with conviction. Two more invitations to testify at congressional hearings came that summer. I returned to the Embassy of Innovation in June to practise opening statements with Max the cat. I turned down the third offer because I needed to study for my oral exams in August to become a PhD candidate. I double-dipped and persuaded Ethan to count both of my written congressional testimonies as two of my written tests. My body reached a level of weariness I had never felt before the night before my oral exam. I felt dizzy, and even walking was difficult. My heart rate increased unexpectedly, as if I were being pursued. I tried taking deep breaths, but they had no effect on settling my nerves. The nonstop travel, exhibitions, and testimonials had proven to be too much to manage in such a short period of time. I rushed to an emergency room near my flat in desperation, wondering if I should cancel the examinations. I imagined the questions my committee members would ask me while dressed in a medical gown. I didn't want to think about my health. After several hours of waiting and a few tests, I was released in the morning with the advice to calm down. "We see too many stressed-out graduate students," a nurse said as I was packing my possessions. I joined a video conference call a few hours later to meet my test committee. I made it through somehow. I was getting closer to finishing this degree. I felt like I was on the right track, but I realised I needed to take better care of myself. I needed every ounce of my strength. Congress was eager to get things done. Follow-up questions came in from both sides of the aisle. The issue of the damaging usage of facial recognition technologies was not limited to one political party. The more lawmakers who can detect the hazards and threats of growing artificial intelligence, the more probable it is that appropriate legislation will be passed. According to accounts from my colleagues in Washington, the success of our hearing was followed by a steady stream of lobbyists visiting various lawmakers. Laura Moy and I kept coming back to resource restrictions as we discussed next steps. Our little organisations just did not have the same amount of time, staff capability, or money to contact politicians on a regular basis as lobbyists do. It was time to hit the streets again. How could we persuade Congress to act and safeguard the interests of businesses rather than ordinary citizens? How could we demonstrate to millions of people what was at stake with AI bias?

CHAPTER 15
BETTING ON CODED BIAS

"Where are my keys?"

"Not here," my glasses case replied.

"Try again later," my coat pocket said. I still hadn't repaired the lining hole.

The time could not have been more inconvenient. Another significant step in my struggle for algorithmic justice occurred approximately a year earlier, in 2018, when Shalini Kantayya's name continued to emerge in my direct conversations on social media sites and various inboxes. She saw my TED talk and was interested in interviewing me for a film project. When I checked into her background, I realised she was the director of Catching the Sun, a climate justice film executive produced by Leonardo DiCaprio. While scrolling through my Netflix account, I noticed the film was available. I then watched her TED lecture and discovered we were both Fulbright Scholars. I decided to respond in writing. She instantly booked a flight to Boston to meet me there. I needed to get some shut-eye. The following day, I was scheduled to conduct an on-camera interview. My quest for my misplaced house and office keys was fruitless. I sought sanctuary with a friend. I took a trip to meet her, and she led me to the back of her well-kept home. She escorted me into a neatly arranged guest bedroom and examined my hips. She delivered a new pair of panties in the morning.

"Don't worry, I haven't worn these yet." She burst out laughing.

"I'm guessing I don't need to bring these back."

While I could replace part of my underwear, I was out of luck with the rest of my attire. The costume I had planned for the shoot was in my apartment. I dressed in the identical clothes and glasses as the day before. I applied oil to my nails as a substitute for a finishing coat and arrived at work without a key. Fortunately, because I had a tendency of misplacing my keys, I knew how to contact the facilities group or Media Lab communications director Alexandra Khan. Alexandra was instrumental in ensuring that Shalini and future crews, photographers, and journalists had full access. She had the master key to my workplace today. My office door was opened just in time for the crew to set up. Shalini and I sat down for the first of many interviews and chats. Steve, a tall, stocky man with black hair pulled back in a bun, ran the camera and asked me to pause between comments so he could make adjustments. My office had been penetrated with illumination and reflectors. Shalini followed me after the interview as I presented a presentation for a lab meeting at the large Civic Media table right outside my office. She made a request after seeing me in my job context: "Can I capture you doing something normal?" "May I record you making coffee?"

"I don't drink coffee."

"Making tea?"

"I prefer not to be shown eating or drinking on film."

"When people see a film they aren't going to connect to the research; they are going to connect to you as a person."

"You can film me selecting my glasses."

I was cautious to reveal more about myself outside of my work as a researcher. Although you might not be able to tell from this book, I am an extremely private person, and the last thing I wanted was a filmmaker following me around in my personal space or at intimate times, especially a filmmaker I had just met. My personal life didn't strike me as particularly intriguing. I spent half of my day looking for misplaced goods. But I did think about what she was saying. Shalini wanted people to regard me as approachable. I'd have to trust her and open out a little more to make the process work. I was still concerned. What if she portrays me negatively? I considered what she would display of me outside the lab with some trepidation. I decided to have her videotape the process of having my hair styled at Simply Erinn's, a salon full of Black ladies. I wanted her to see who I talked to about my research outside of the lab and where I found a sense of broader community outside of academic settings. I wondered if I had made the wrong decision as she asked the stylists unpleasant questions about the Black hair industry. I gave the stylists a sheepish look, attempting to convey that she was safe to converse to. Shalini was particularly brave. Throughout our months of shooting, I saw her appear in a variety of settings with me to convey a growing story with no apparent finish in sight. The process might not always be comfortable, but it was vital to be willing to go through the awkward moments and blunders. My journey to becoming more open on-screen began in the stylist's chair, with my hair as unfinished as the story Shalini was creating. I didn't have any laptops or screens to hide behind in that chair. If we wanted people to regard me as more than just a researcher, we'd start at the beginning. If I truly believed that humanity was at the centre of computing, I would need to become more comfortable with displaying my own humanity and overcome my fear of losing credibility and respect if I was not always polished. I continued the talk on algorithmic prejudice with half my hair out in an Afro and the other half expertly twisted by Ranae, my go-to stylist. Under the roar of a hair dryer, I called out to Shalini, "I hope this is intimate enough for you."

By the summer of 2019, the project, like so many other independent documentaries, had run out of financing. Shalini accompanied me to Atlantic Towers Plaza, but before shooting the Brooklyn tenants and me, she admitted that she didn't have enough money to record more footage. I attended a meeting where I spoke with a communications specialist who had been brought in particularly to assist NGOs. I told her about the documentary's continued development, my enthusiasm for the subject, and the need for extra assistance. She looked at me with sympathy, given all the work and chances on my plate, and questioned, "Are you sure this documentary is really worth your time?"

Was she correct? Was I squandering my time? It had been about a year, and there was no sign of an end in sight. I responded by saying, "It will be worth the time if we make the investment to support it."

She was not the ally I had hoped for at the time. The moment made it clear to me that I was taking a risk by devoting my efforts to the unfinished documentary. I believed the risk was worthwhile even before there was anything to show for it other than expenditure reports since Shalini was capturing critical stories about algorithmic harm that needed to be conveyed. Unlike many well-funded efforts about difficulties in the tech ecosystem, her documentary focused on people of colour. What was obvious to me was not so obvious to others. In the face of doubt, I had to believe in myself. The film's objective was to expose the coded gaze, and I needed to bet on Shalini, myself, and the severity of what we were presenting. I hoped that if this film was ever produced, it would effectively personalise the consequences of AI bias and make the dangers of AI a topic for many people to discuss. Unfortunately, if we wait for rapid results before investing time, talent, treasure, and networks in creative projects, they may never receive the support they require to grow. When the film's finances were at their lowest, I contacted Doron Weber of the Alfred P. Sloan Foundation. Doron Weber had the foresight to award a $50,000 writing grant to Margot Lee Shetterly, author of the book Hidden Figures, which was later adapted into the inspirational film. I found out about this backstory after I posted my thoughts on the film and my work on algorithmic bias on the Rhodes Scholar email group. I recall going to a film showing at MIT when Margot gave a presentation. I was moved to tears as I sat in a bouncing blue chair at the Kendall Square Cinema, watching Black women walk together toward more opportunities. I was astonished by how much emotional impact witnessing technical, analytical, and bright Black women on film had on me. I'd become accustomed to seeing a few people who looked like me performing the kind of work I do. I left the Hidden Figures screening room with a deep understanding that representation is critical, and that telling stories that are frequently hidden or rarely elevated not only corrected the historical record, but also allowed others to see within themselves the possibility of making contributions that broader society would say were beyond their reach, scope, intelligence, or capability. Intellectually, I recognized the importance of role models. Hidden Figures elevated that understanding from an intellectual recognition to a visceral experience. We are capable and necessary, both then and today. I received a copy of the book months later. I discovered a handwritten statement on the first few pages: "Congratulations on winning the search for the Hidden Figures contest, and thanks for accepting the torch from these women." The gift was completed by Margot's signature, the echo of her hand conveying the torch of encouragement to me. Doron and I had met on a mailing group a few years before, so I contacted him to inform him that the video was underfunded but made a big impact. He agreed to see Shalini. I made the introduction in the spring of 2019, shortly after leaving the

Atlantic Towers complex, when we were visiting the Brooklyn renters. It was now up to Shalini's tenacity and persuasion to turn the warm lead into resources. Despite numerous denials, the Sloan Foundation came through, providing critical funds to help bring the project to completion. Funding is required, yet it is insufficient. The picture was yet to be completed, and the frantic rush to the end could have been a film in its own right. Shalini informed me just before Thanksgiving in 2019 that the film has been accepted into Sundance! I didn't know the difference between Sundance and Moonpie at the time; all I knew was that Shalini was ecstatic. "Joy, this is the film festival where the leading studios and distributors come to choose films to purchase," she stated over the phone. A Sundance premiere is the ideal way for a small documentary like ours to reach a huge audience."

"It appears that I should make plans to go. "Where is it being held?"

"Park City, Utah."

"When is it?"

"January."

There were a few more obstacles to overcome before we could prepare our snow boots. The film lacked a title. We weren't delighted with the working title Code for Bias, but more importantly, the film didn't have a conclusion. I informed Shalini that the Brooklyn tenants had made substantial headway in their fight against their landlord's installation of a facial recognition entry system. I forwarded her links to related articles, such as "Brooklyn Landlord Does an About Face on Facial Recognition Plan" and "How We Fought Our Landlord's Secretive Plan for Facial Recognition—and Won." As Shalini decided to continue that storyline, it remained to be seen how the film would end. The picture was not directed or produced by me. The film would be distributed by Women Make Movies and sold by Shalini's production firm, 7th Empire. My behind-the-scenes attempts to financially sponsor the film and persuade my collaborators to participate did not give me control over how the story was conveyed. The Algorithmic Justice League would not receive any proceeds from the film, nor would I or any of the film's cast be compensated for our participation. This was a significant labour of love.

Documentaries are often made over many years, rather than in the month-to-month sprints we had just completed. To get the documentary ready for Sundance, everyone involved had to work double shifts. Shalini and Steve with the bun arrived in Boston to film the last shots. We scheduled a video call with Tranae and Icemae. I created a poem that I wished to share with them in order to celebrate their bravery and example.

Unlike the first time Steve and Shalini visited Boston, I had my keys and a whole wardrobe. I grabbed numerous outfits, a few pairs of spectacles, the AJL shield, and polished my newly purchased double monk-strap dress shoes. Then I went to the shoot venue, which was a coworking space I was renting for AJL. We looted the open kitchen, which had goodies waiting for us. Today we wouldn't have to spend as much money on lunch. We had enough variation by switching rooms in the coworking space to look to have travelled to several locales. We reset cameras and lighting equipment on other floors, keeping in mind that Shalini and Steve had a flight that day. In November 2019, there was a lot to be thankful for, but returning borrowed production equipment from the shoot to the MIT Media Lab was not at the top of my list. It was exhausting to walk three blocks. I waved to Shalini and Steve as they drove by in a car in a last-minute bid to catch their early-evening flights. I hadn't signed up to be a member of the production team, but at this stage, everyone was chipping in to help get the job done. The wheelchair ramp on the side of the Media Lab was a welcome sight; it made transporting the equipment back to my office easier. Time would tell if the back pain and year-end craziness were worth it.

The Sundance Film Festival kicked up on January 23, 2020, my thirty-first birthday. My journey from the lab to the corridors of Congress, from graduate student to founder of the Algorithmic Justice League, will soon be in the limelight of the documentary world, several years after I first coding in a white mask. We walked the red carpet with the crew and cast, taking photos while wearing black square sunglasses that resembled censorship strips to represent opposing face monitoring. I could feel more and more eyes on me, but I wasn't fully at ease in the spotlight. I decided not to overdress because I was uncomfortable as the film's major protagonist. Thinking back on the harsh comments to my TED Talk, I questioned if a film like this would further fuel the naysayers. On the other side, I remembered how many individuals had contacted me and told me that my work made them feel seen. The spotlight both shins and burns, and my duty tonight was to concentrate on the shine. Our team stepped into a completely packed theatre to greet the debut of what we eventually termed Coded Bias. I observed both the movie and the audience. I was overjoyed as the audience applauded a slow-motion sequence of me buckling my shining shoes, sliding a red ring on my pointer finger, and finishing the appearance with the AJL shield strapped to my back. I noticed people leaning forward in their seats, taking in the stories of the excoded.

Individuals or communities affected by algorithmic systems are excoded. People like Daniel Santos, a schoolteacher who received low scores from an automated system despite earning multiple "Teacher of the Year" awards, were among the excoded. "For a moment I doubted myself...then I realised the algorithm is a lie," he said to a stunned crowd. By the end of the video, audience members were brimming with questions for Shalini and myself about what they had just observed. The energy was akin to what I had sensed at the Hidden Figures screening years before. There was astonishment and pride in the air. I felt really pleased and blessed to have been able to contribute to the creation of a film that prompted people to reconsider their ideas about AI's capabilities. Doron was sitting in the rear corner of a booth at the after-party in a basement pub. He congratulated me and added, "This is one of the best investments we've ever made in a science documentary." I was curious if he stated this about all of his documentaries. I decided to put on a brave front and give him the benefit of the doubt.

Coded Bias was televised nationally on PBS through Independent Lens a year after its world premiere at Sundance. The television station that had transported my nine-year-old imagination into MIT now showed me discussing artificial intelligence at MIT. Perhaps another child saw me and imagined new possibilities. Coded Bias was available on Netflix to its more than 200 million users shortly after its PBS debut and was translated into thirty languages. The film got widespread praise and multiple accolades.

CHAPTER 16
COSTS OF INCLUSION AND EXCLUSION

In the run-up to the satellite media tour and the taping of the Good Morning America feature, I collaborated with the Olay team on press release and campaign website materials. After being reminded of the agony of erasure, I began to consider how I could use this media spotlight to highlight the critical work of others. I added a reference to Dr. Safiya Noble's work, author of Algorithms of Oppression, whose groundbreaking study on racial and gender prejudice in search engines forcefully revealed how Black girls and women of colour were portrayed in unflattering ways. Searches for "Black girls" or "Asian girls" yielded hypersexualized and occasionally pornographic images, whereas searches for "White girls" yielded no comparable top results. The resource section included her book, as well as work by leading feminist thinkers, such as Dr. Ruha Benjamin's Race After Technology and Dr. Sasha Costanza-Chock's Design Justice—the book that gave me a better understanding of the harms and erasure that trans people face, and broadened my thinking about how to reach people of all genders with a beauty campaign. In addition to highlighting the work of great thinkers, I proposed that Olay include Black Girls CODE to help them achieve their goal of increasing the number of women of colour in STEM. They both agreed! The campaign's call to action would be to use the hashtag #DecodeTheBias on social media to send females to coding camp. This effort also aided AJL's strategic goal of elevating the excoded, or those who are damaged by AI systems. I wasn't sure how much I could affect the campaign, and I was concerned about the idea of being forced to provide lines. I didn't believe it. I was sceptical. When Play first approached me, I presented their idea to the AJL board members for feedback. Overall, board members saw the potential for reach, but we also felt that the framing needed to be changed. We discussed how much information can be delivered in a sixty-second ad and, given the limits, what was most crucial to highlight. I was shocked when Olay and Madonna Badger asked me to join their team as a creative partner and collaborator. They handed me paperwork explaining the commercial's creative elements and encouraged my lyrical voice to be included in the script. One of the early versions of the campaign was built on the concept of inclusion and collecting face images to help improve the performance of Olay's Skin Advisor system. We debated the topic, "Code me into what?" after some back-and-forth about how being coded in without explicit agency could really put people up for surveillance. Nonetheless, the Olay team pointed out that in my TED-featured lecture, I advocated for a "Selfies for Inclusion" initiative to combat algorithmic bias. They were correct: I had proposed what appeared to be the simplest approach to eliminate algorithmic bias: producing more inclusive datasets. I had caved in to well-meaning pressure to close my lecture with something that people could do, so that I wasn't merely a bearer of bad news. At that point in my development, I believed in my proclivity for action. To an engineer, action meant producing something; hence, when faced with a technical difficulty, my initial response was to devise a technical solution: create a better dataset. However, when it comes to the implementation of facial recognition technology in the real world, we're dealing with a sociotechnical issue, which is a departure from my computer science background. When dealing with a sociotechnical challenge, code and data are insufficient since the difficulties transcend beyond how well a specific system operates and, more importantly, how a system will be used. Who will gain? Who will suffer? Who gets to make the call? These were issues of power, not of performance measurements. In 2016, I wrote an article on my TEDxBeaconStreet talk, in which I battled with the tension between alternative ways to eliminate algorithmic prejudice.

As much as the engineer in me wants simple answers and technical solutions, the reality is considerably more complex. In the design and implementation of AI systems, there are costs of inclusion and costs of exclusion that must be considered. Consider the cost of exclusion. A blanket rejection of AI systems that analyse humans in some way will prevent good innovations from taking place. AI systems, for example, are increasingly being used in medical diagnoses. After surviving breast cancer, Dr. Regina Barzilay of MIT used her expertise and personal experience to develop AI algorithms that have shown great promise in detecting early indicators of the disease. I was encouraged to hear a group of researchers from the healthcare start-up Ubenwa use machine learning to analyse the cries of babies in Nigeria to diagnose lung issues at a Black in AI session. However, there is strong evidence that AI systems developed with benign purposes can produce biassed results in the medical environment. Stanford researchers published a report in 2017 that demonstrated encouraging results for skin cancer diagnosis using computer vision. They were able to match dermatologists' performance, and joyful headlines followed. However, the dataset used to test the performance was eventually discovered to be mainly composed of people with lighter skin. So far, this investigation has taken a somewhat technical approach to the topic. A sociotechnical perspective requires us to consider not only datasets but also the social factors that led to a preference for white skin in dermatology and how medical apartheid shows itself. While serving as a judge for a Mozilla competition, I was introduced to the term medical apartheid. Avery Smith was one of the applicants who received funding. He wrote movingly about the death of his wife from melanoma. The cancer had grown beyond repair by the time she was diagnosed, and her tale mirrored the trend of dark-skinned persons being diagnosed with skin cancer at far later stages. One aspect of the issue is medical education. Many medical textbooks and tests feature light-skinned portrayals of dermatological disorders, exposing medical students to relatively limited representations of the condition by the time they become clinicians. Another difficulty in therapeutic settings is gender and racial bias. The disregard of patient worries about their health, particularly the pain of patients of colour, women, and women of colour, also implies that even if we do seek medical attention, our symptoms and discomfort may be discounted or underestimated. Other aspects of the problem include a dearth of dermatologists with whom patients feel they can relate, as well as justified suspicion of the healthcare system in light of historical injustices. To solve these challenges, Avery founded Melalogic, which addresses both the social and technical sides of the problem of dark-skinned individuals failing to receive critical dermatological care on time. On the social front, the company was building a database of Black dermatologists to help patients find someone to whom they might relate. On the technical side, it meant compiling more cases of dermatological problems on darker skin. Avery's work, inspired by a profound personal tragedy, illustrates the way forward in developing future AI systems that address social, cultural, and historical issues. The expenses of inclusion are on the other side of the equation. While more diversified dermatology datasets can aid in the reduction of medical apartheid, inclusion can have drawbacks. Because my research on algorithmic prejudice was prompted by facial recognition technology (FRTs), I was forced to deal with the consequences of inclusion right away. Diversifying datasets to improve FRT performance in a vacuum may appear to be a simple solution to algorithmic bias. However, algorithmic bias—when a system performs better on one group than another—is simply one aspect of the topic. When we consider algorithmic justice—shifting power so that the responsibilities of technology do not fall on the disadvantaged and the benefits do not accrue solely to the privileged few—we must also consider algorithmic harm. Even if FRTs were theoretically perfect, more precise systems may be misused. They can be enlisted to build a surveillance-ready state. They may be programmed to distinguish not just a person's unique biometric signature, but also soft biometrics such as age. Technology that can predict demographic or phenotypic features with some accuracy can be used to profile individuals, making particular groups more prone to unjustified police stops. According to The Intercept, IBM used covert surveillance footage from the New York Police NYPD and provided the NYPD with tools to search for persons in video by hair colour, skin tone, and facial hair. Such capabilities raise concerns about police racial profiling automation. Police brutality, which can be exacerbated by the advancement of surveillance technologies such as facial recognition, which can in turn erode civil rights and liberties, is a life-taking and life-threatening harm that goes beyond technical algorithmic prejudice. Consideration of broad algorithmic damages, rather than particular algorithmic bias, is required to overcome what the nonprofit think tank Data & Society refers to as the "specification dilemma." People who might be affected by misidentification, for example, can be accounted for when adverse implications are narrowly defined to focus on technical performance of facial recognition systems, but the impact of mass monitoring falls outside this concept. It's crucial to remember, as I wrote for The New York Times, that even if false-positive match rates improve, improper use of face recognition technology cannot be remedied with a software patch. Even precise facial recognition can be utilised in unsettling ways. Face recognition technology was used by the

Baltimore police department to identify and arrest persons who participated in the 2015 protests against police wrongdoing in the aftermath of Freddie Gray's death in Baltimore. We must oppose the increasing usage of this technology.

So by the time I was talking to someone about perhaps gathering photographs for the Olay campaign, I had a better idea of what I was doing. I have a lot more expertise recognizing the problems caused by facial recognition technology that were caused by more than just performance issues. I also have more tools to work with than just my engineering talents. I testified in favour of a government moratorium on FRTs. I had backed effective anti-FRT resistance campaigns. I'd also postponed the launch of a face data tagging project I'd been working on for months. I had also received a lot of backlash for the TEDxBeaconStreet call to action. The final call to action looked at who was generating technology rather than how it was developed by sending girls to code camp instead of collecting selfie photographs. Sending girls to code camp was a first step toward tackling structural factors that contributed to algorithmic bias and attractiveness bias. To combat beauty prejudice, we required more "women leading and coding their beautiful ideas."

We also required more companies to step forward and perform algorithmic audits on their AI solutions. The #DecodeTheBias campaign concluded with an assessment of Olay's Skin Advisor tool. When I was first requested to audit the tool, I informed the team that given what I knew about how it was created, there was a good chance we'd find unflattering bias. I also did not want to be a part of an audit whose results would not be made public. The Olay team refused to back down. "If we find bias in our tool, we will do what it takes to fix it."

"What if it cannot be fixed?" I wondered.

Olay responded, "If there is no way to make it more just and inclusive, we will shut it down." I was taken aback.

The option of not proceeding or stopping the construction of a system was rarely available. "All right, if you really want to do the audit and we agree in writing that we can publish the results, I can help you with all pieces of the campaign." Following our discussion with Olay, I called my blue-haired freedom fighter Cathy O'Neil, the founder of the algorithmic auditing firm ORCAA. "What do you know about skin care?"

"Basically nothing."

"No worries, I have an epic audit we should do."

"Tell me more."

The ORCAA investigation found that the Skin Advisor app has algorithmic bias based on skin colour and age. Our findings were published on the companion website dedicated to the #DecodeTheBias campaign. Importantly, I had ultimate editorial control over the report, which ensured that even negative results were disseminated. P&G went one step further by pledging to take actions that addressed our proposal by a specific date. The most crucial action, in my opinion, was their agreement to the Consented Data Promise, which commits them to using only data gathered with express user consent. I got the term from the Olay Skin Promise (zero skin retouching in all advertisements). The corporation had stopped airbrushing models and spokesmen by the time I was the face of this campaign. The photographs and videos in the ad were recorded without the use of blemish-removal procedures in post-production. While I liked the Skin Promise's intention, I was secretly disappointed. I wanted to know that if I had a pimple at the wrong time, the airbrush would save me. Knowing I had no backup, I embarked on a "beauty bootcamp." For vanity's sake, I did everything perfectly. I drank mostly water and avoided all caffeinated beverages. I exercised five times per week and went to bed at a reasonable hour, getting an average of eight hours of sleep per night. And, of course, I used the Olay skin care items that were displayed on my sink. Eye creams, face creams, serums, clay masks, and a cucumber-scented mist.

Having organisations endure public-facing audits, like knowing I couldn't hide behind post-production retouching, can impose positive pressure. While Olay requested the audit voluntarily, we cannot assume that all corporations would do the same. While there may be some decent actors, relying on the tech industry's benevolence and moral impulses is not a responsible or reliable strategy. The year following the Olay ad, I witnessed firsthand the necessity for government agencies to be pressed to test technology from startups selling AI services. For the time being, with beauty bootcamp finished, it was time to return to my PhD. My time off had cost me money. I had hoped that anyone who saw the campaign's magazine ads would notice "Dr. Joy Buolamwini, Founder of the Algorithmic Justice League and Poet of Code." I had not yet acquired the honorific because I had missed my defence date. The most discouraging aspect of the process was contacting the PR company for the campaign and instructing them to remove the "Dr." title from the press release and print advertisements.

I was lucky to have a glam team assigned to prepare me for the satellite media trip when the campaign eventually began. Amy, a tall Nigerian woman, did my cosmetics. When I showed her the print advertisement, she looked at me with tears in her eyes. "I know it's supposed to be for little girls, but it's also for me." We don't often see ourselves celebrated in this way." Her reaction instilled in me the joy of belonging. I didn't need another certification to make others feel seen or taken seriously.

CHAPTER 17
CUPS OF HOPE

On miniature Great Seals of the United States adorning a collection of cupcakes, eagle claws held a bundle of arrows and an olive branch. The cupcakes stood guard outside a room teeming with excitement about the White House event. Fabian Rogers spoke from behind a podium on his experience as a Brooklyn renter against the installation of facial recognition technology in his apartment building. He spoke to a crowd seated on blue-backed chairs for the long-awaited launch. The White House was poised to unveil a Blueprint for an AI Bill of Rights in the fall of 2022 after significant consultation. There was finally one document created from several sources. It is said, "E Pluribus Unum."

My footsteps boomed across a lengthy corridor in the massive Eisenhower Executive Office Building, near to the White House, before I reached my seat. The halls reminded me of the Rayburn Building, which hosted congressional hearings. As a student, I testified twice before a committee about the societal implications of artificial intelligence. Every time I left, I worried if those hearings had any effect. I came without knowing what would happen because I felt obligated to share what my study had shown. I felt a responsibility to the Brooklyn tenants I had vowed to assist. I had made a vow to fight against AI dangers with the excoded. Today, I saw the results of years of activism by so many organisations and individuals prepared to speak out against the dangers of AI in a world fascinated with the promises. Tawana Petty, one of those people, sat next to me, her cane resting on her right leg and purple-tinted glasses perched on her nose.

While my childhood fascination with robots and my academic articles had led me to the struggle for algorithmic justice as an AI researcher, Tawana had taken a different road, with an often overlooked but crucial perspective. As a mother and concerned Detroit resident, she began to consider the impact of technology on her city. Her interest and concern about efforts such as Project Greenlight, a citywide surveillance effort, spurred her involvement. We connected via our mutual love of poetry and our growing concern about the potentially destructive usage of AI systems. She formally joined the Algorithmic Justice League in 2022. Before she became our senior policy and advocacy advisor, she knew what it was like to struggle to make ends meet, to be homeless, and to be an organiser. She used to tell me, "I am highly educated, not highly schooled." I like that statement because it reminds me that while certifications and degrees are important, they are not required to learn about the effects of technology or to advocate for change. To make an impact in the fight for algorithmic justice, you don't need a PhD from MIT. All that is required is a curious mind and a human heart.

You don't have to understand how biometric technologies work to understand that when they are used for mass monitoring and invasion of privacy, they do not make us safer by default. You don't have to understand what a neural net is to realise that if an AI system rejects you for a job based on your ethnicity, gender, age, disability, or skin colour, something is wrong. You don't have to be an AI researcher to understand that if firms use your creative work to make products without your permission or remuneration, you have been harmed.

What we need to know is that our intellectual rights will be preserved, and that no corporation claiming to be responsible or ethical will be able to sell items based on unauthorised data. What we need to know is that our biometric data, such as our facial data and the distinct sound of our voices, will be safeguarded. Multiple communities around the United States have set restrictions on law enforcement's use of face recognition technology, which has often landed innocent people, particularly Black males, in jail. Federal biometric safeguards are required in the United States and around the world. Following a public outrage when the Internal Revenue Service used an outside corporation to authenticate taxpayers' faces, the agency stated that it would no longer use third parties for access to core government services. We must hold them to that pledge so that no one has to give up their face in order to receive benefits or access veteran services. We should not have to hand over sensitive information to third-party firms in exchange for the right to sue, even if we have no choice but to utilise their products. We do not have to believe that once AI technologies have been implemented, they cannot be reversed. We do not have to assume that just because a company has made a product, it is a given that the product will be used. In Italy, regulators halted ChatGPT due to privacy concerns following a data leak. They punished Clearview AI for illegally scraping billions of face pictures, and they ordered that the faces of Italian people be erased from their computers. We can go even farther and mandate that all companies developing AI systems based on personally identifiable information provide proof of consent and erase any ill-gotten data as well as the AI models produced with unconsented data.

We can request face purges and complete data removals. In a legal dispute over its use of face data submitted by Facebook users, Meta removed over a billion faceprints and agreed to a $650 million settlement. This case was made feasible by the Illinois Biometric Information Privacy Act, which makes it illegal in the state to use biometric information without authorization. Litigation and public outrage, as well as legislation, make an impact. We require legislation. Draft legislation addressing algorithmic responsibility, remote biometric technology, and data privacy has been introduced over the years. With more people becoming aware of the impact of artificial intelligence on our lives, we need to know that our government institutions will protect our civil rights regardless of how technology progresses.

The AI Bill of Rights was created to present a positive vision for the kind of safeguards required to preserve civil rights as the creation and acceptance of AI systems grows. AI systems must be safe and effective, data privacy must be maintained, and automated systems must not perpetuate illegal discrimination. These reasonable safeguards must be both asserted and applied. The AI Bill of Rights, released as a template and playbook to provide real examples for implementation, provides a stepping stone toward much-needed legislation—the kind of legislation that would lead to systemic change, so we wouldn't have to rely on corporations' voluntary good behaviour.

I looked across the room as I greeted the news of the AI Bill of Rights. Representatives from the National Institute of Standards and Technology sat in front of me and across the aisle. I'd visited the NIST website frequently to help with my research, and it felt like I was seeing characters from an old book. NIST would produce an AI Risk Management Framework in January 2023, outlining steps enterprises might take to prevent AI damages and discrimination in their products. These collaborative efforts gave me hope. Recognizing the existence of an issue is the first step toward resolving it. People used to wonder if algorithmic bias existed or if machines might discriminate in detrimental ways because they were intended to be "objective."

The AI Bill of Rights inaugural event included a panel discussion with federal officials from the Departments of Education, Health and Human Services, the Equal Employment Opportunity Commission, and the Consumer Financial Protection Bureau. The panellists spoke as if the dangers of AI were obvious: "We know AI can perpetuate bias." I also recall feeling a unique connection when Dr. Alondra Nelson, the acting director of the White House Office of Science and Technology Policy, addressed the podium and described the inspiration for this collaborative effort. When we hugged, our temples linked and rested for a time. Her hug seemed like an endorsement and a thank you for your persistence in raising awareness about the dangers of AI. I hope she sensed my respect for her leadership.

In Europe, too, hope was on the rise. The EU AI Act was being debated. If passed, it will establish a precedent for how artificial intelligence will be managed not just in the European Union, but around the world. Algorithmic risk assessments and AI audits, such as the one I conducted for the "Gender Shades" project, would be required when AI systems were utilised in high-risk contexts such as law enforcement, employment, and education. As a member of the African diaspora, I cannot forget that AI damages are felt in the Global South, and all too often, those bearing the consequences are the ones who are least represented in choosing the local and international regulations that govern their usage. So many of the discussions and deliberations I've had about how to prevent AI risks have focused on the interests of the Global North. The Distributed Artificial Intelligence Research (DAIR) Institute has been particularly vociferous about the need to disseminate AI resources and research outside a few giant tech enterprises. In May 2023, more than 150 individuals that provide content moderation and data detoxification services assembled in Nairobi, Kenya. They voted to establish the first African Content Moderators Union. Though often left out of global discourse, many of the Kenyan workers are paid less than $2.00 an hour to go through trauma-inducing content for products like ChatGPT, TikTok, and Facebook. Their move to unionise and call attention to the lack of mental health care, low pay, and unpredictable work is a vital step in addressing exploitative practices that enable headline-grabbing AI technologies.

The work toward algorithmic justice must not be just worldwide; it must also be intergenerational. The next generation is making gains with youth-led organisations like Encode Justice, which is focused on establishing a movement for human-centred AI with members spanning thirty nations in both high school and college. We joined with Encode Justice as the AJL began to establish a harm-reporting platform for common people to share their stories and seek support. We started by focusing on the use of AI systems in schools for anything from automated grading to teacher assessments and exam proctoring. We extended to collect reports from taxpayers trying to access key government services, travellers feeling obliged to submit to face scans, and more. In addition to our efforts, governments around the world must maintain AI incident-reporting mechanisms that document known issues with AI systems in order to enable future learning and prevention. We must also implement restitution systems so that if someone is harmed by an AI technology, they may seek assistance from relevant government agencies. Through my employment, I meet people and organisations who are dedicated to preventing AI harms. My employment brings me into contact with organisations that are developing ethical AI systems and actively researching methods to improve them. There is a burgeoning ecosystem of digital justice organisations, equity-minded research facilities, and education efforts that are gaining momentum, collecting evidence, and raising awareness about the hazards that AI promises.

The work continues thanks to organisations like AJL and DAIR, which are led by people who have lived through the effects of AI and are devoted to fighting alongside the excoded. But we can't do it without your help.

If you have a face, you have a place in the conversation and the decisions that affect your everyday life—decisions that are rapidly being impacted by growing artificial intelligence technologies. We need your voice because, in the end, we decide what type of world we want to live in. We do not have to tolerate situations and customs that make it difficult for us to live dignified lives. We do not have to stand by and watch liberation movements for racial equality, gender equality, workers' rights, disability rights, immigrant rights, and so many others see their gains undermined by the hasty adoption of artificial intelligence, which promises efficiency but further automates inequality.

The rising frontier in the fight for civil and humanitarian rights will require algorithmic justice, which for me ultimately means that people have a voice and a choice in determining and shaping the algorithmic decisions that shape their lives, that when harms are perpetuated by AI systems, there is accountability in the form of redress to correct the harms inflected, and that we do not settle on notions of fairness that do not

Tawana and I got some cupcakes on our way out of the Executive Office Building after the launch ceremony. We came to a halt at the top of the Navy Steps, which face the White House. For a brief moment, we stood, little figures on glittering stone, still willing to trust that our tomorrows will be better than our yesterdays—a conviction inspired not by machines and technological development, but by the endurance and ingenuity of ordinary people. The future of AI is uncertain. Will we allow a few digital companies to wield authority over our lives? Will we strive for a society that protects all people's rights? Will we dare to believe in our own and our country's power? Will we march to the rhythm of justice? It is ultimately up to us to find the answers.

— we have finished our cupcakes and refuelled to continue the fight for algorithm justice.

The contents of this book may not be copied, reproduced or transmitted without the express written permission of the author or publisher. Under no circumstances will the publisher or author be responsible or liable for any damages, compensation or monetary loss arising from the information contained in this book, whether directly or indirectly. .

Disclaimer Notice:

Although the author and publisher have made every effort to ensure the accuracy and completeness of the content, they do not, however, make any representations or warranties as to the accuracy, completeness, or reliability of the content. , suitability or availability of the information, products, services or related graphics contained in the book for any purpose. Readers are solely responsible for their use of the information contained in this book

Every effort has been made to make this book possible. If any omission or error has occurred unintentionally, the author and publisher will be happy to acknowledge it in upcoming versions.

Copyright © 2023

All rights reserved.

Printed in Great Britain
by Amazon